My Name Is Victory

Julie Keene Ballard & Lisa Daughdrill

Full Circle Publishing
Amarillo, TX

Full Circle Publishing
PO Box 1144
Amarillo, TX 79105

First Paperback edition February 2017

Designs by Chris Boe, our Brother in Christ, Friend, & Anointed One

Manufactured in the United States of America

Scriptures referred to in this book are taken from the most up to date translation of the Holy Bible published by Zondervan Publishing House and provided online by biblegateway.com. Take note that the name satan and related names are not capitalized. We choose not to acknowledge him, even to the point of violating grammatical rules.

ISBN-13: 978-0692833018

ISBN-10: 0692833013

—

Dedication

Julie's Dedication:

I dedicate this book to my Mom, Phyllis Freeman, who has never left my side but still gave me hard love when I needed it the most. It is because of your diligent prayers and your faithfulness to God, your trust in Him, and your love for me, that I am alive today to share the GOOD NEWS!

To my Dad, Mike Freeman, who has been the solid, tangible, ROCK that God blessed us with. You put our family back together with your instant, unconditional love that has lasted trial after trial with the women you took on as the provider and hope for our family. Our lives are so much better because you came! Thank you, Dad, for all that you do for us!

To my sisters, the 3 women that I have walked beside, cried with, and loved. Jessie, Kathryn, and Emily, you three are all so very different, but each of you add something unto me that cannot be replaced. The love that you have shown me, even in my darkest moments, have been rays of sunshine that have lit up even the most treacherous paths. Thank you for never giving up on me, even though the hurt I inflicted upon each of you was unbearable.

To my children far away, you are forever on my heart and as long as I have breath in me, you are fought for, sought after, and loved. I will cherish you both until the end of time and nothing will be able to separate the bond that we share even across the miles and distance between us. My heart beats for you daily and I will hold in my heart the sweet moments we shared, forever.

Lisa's Dedication:

This book is dedicated to my Husband, David E. Daughdrill, my Boaz, my gift who loves me, protects and provides, strengthens and leads me in the ways of the Lord. Your heart blows me away. God bless you.

To my Mother, Bonnie McCaskell-Wiggins and her husband Paul Wiggins who stand in the gap and in agreement praying for me every single day. I feel your love and so appreciate those prayers. God bless you.

To my Sister and biggest Cheerleader, Tami McCaskell Edwards and her husband, Coach Brian Edwards, without your constant encouragement and unwavering generous love I would not be where I am today, in my mind or my life. God bless you.

And especially to my amazing first-born Son, Justin Wade Byrd, there are not adequate words to say what you mean to me. You are a grace gift, one I never deserved, but a beautiful gift God so lavishly blessed me with. The instant I met you, you showed me what His mercy is, what real love is, unconditional, everlasting love. Our hearts have always beat in sync. I dedicate not only this book but my life so that you may always be free. I adore you son and thank you for loving me. God bless you my child.

—

Forward

I have learned a VERY valuable life lesson – and that lesson is – that when I find my back against the wall, my poor choices in life haunting me, my life going down the toilet – there is one place I can always go to get the best advice on how to get back on the right track. And that place is at the feet of an "OVERCOMER." Webster's definition of an "overcomer" is - One who has gained VICTORY over a deep personal struggle or conflict in life – **A CONQUEROR.** I want solid experienced advice on how to climb out of the muck and mire I have found myself in from someone who has already successfully done it – not somebody that's just read about it. I want advice from someone who has successfully made that one way trip from the Pit of Hell to the Gates of Heaven.

The authors of this book Julie Keene Ballard and Lisa Daughdrill have both made that journey and in my opinion deserve the Title of "OVERCOMER."

If you have found yourself in that place where you are saying to yourself: "I just can't live like this anymore" but you don't have any idea on how to get free from what is trying to take you out – THEN READ THIS BOOK!

Pastor Charlie Haynes/Senior Pastor and Founder of:
Righteous Oaks Recovery Center for Men
Jacob's Well Recovery Center for Women
Damascus Road Recovery Center for Men
www.jacobswellrecoverycenter.com

It is an honor and a privilege to have the opportunity to forward this book, "My Name is Victory", which is written by some awesome women of God the Lord has blessed me to connect with in friendship and fellowship in Christ! They are a blessing to me in my life just by knowing and serving with them in the kingdom and seeing God's hands on their lives. It is awesome to see what God is doing in them as they have been a great motivation and inspiration to me as well as others through their phenomenal love for Christ which is manifested in their desire to help others.

Author and Co-Author, Sister Julie Keene Ballard, has experienced firsthand and has walked a mile in many of our shoes. God has gifted her to publish many books and in doing so, helps others fulfill their dreams by utilizing her passion in her expertise in the ministry of help service. Author Julie Keene Ballard has touched on some powerful key points with her victorious testimony. This book expounds on the struggle of addiction, the agony of defeat, as well as the triumphant victory in Christ. Julie's testimony of recovery in itself is a highlight of victory in Christ that will inspire anyone who struggles with any addiction. In this book you will find out that is not how you fall down, it is how you get up.

Proverbs 24:16 - Though a righteous man falls seven times, he rises again.

What does it mean to be a winner? What drives you to success? What gives you the determination to get back up and get on with things? We all fall down from time to time. If we say that we don't, then we deceive ourselves. Many people have been knocked down, and many people have been kicked so hard and have fallen so low, that they have wondered how they can ever get back up from such a blow. For some, it is the pain of separation from a loved one, the loss of a loved one, or even a divorce. For some, it is the pain of personal betrayal. For others, perhaps the loss of a job, the heart ache of failure, or having their dreams broken. For some, it is the awful feeling - that gut wrenching, guilty feeling of sinning and letting God down. For some it may be the pressures of life that satan uses to weaken the faith of his believers. This book is a testament that Jesus Christ can bring total victory to your life no matter what your story looks like. God will give you Victory. The Co-Author, Julie Keene Ballard, has inspired me to pursue my dreams as Author. She is definitely a gift from God to inspire others through her story as Co-Author with Pastor Lisa Daughdrill, my spiritual daughter.

Lisa has first-hand experience with grief in the loss of her beloved son through the comfort of the Holy Spirit. She teaches on this topic of how you can spirituality overcome grief through the power of God's Word. It is her endeavor in ministering and counseling that has helped many by imparting hope and restoration in the lives of men and women in recovery that have experienced addiction and grief. I have seen firsthand the love and passion she has for God's people in of all walks of life. This book is a testament of the heart they each have in Christ. This is for anyone looking for total victory.

Isaiah 53:3 - He is despised and rejected by men; a man of sorrows, and acquainted with grief: and we hid as it were our faces from him; he was despised, and we esteemed him not.

God is raising up people with a testimony that will assist and help others to rise and live victorious. This book is a must read. You, too, can have victory in your life through the power of Jesus Christ. It is my prayer that this book reaches the nations. I encourage anyone who needs victory to read this inspiration that will help in every area of your life.

Having had a spiritual awakening as the result of this testimony, they are to carry it now to the nations, to witness to the power of this message to anyone, and to practice these principles in all our affairs, to serve faithful under the inspiration of the Holy Spirit serving Jesus Christ as Lord.

Pastor Carl Flowers
Apostle – Trinity Outreach Ministries – Picayune, MS
Author – "From Sin & Shame to Glory", "Finish Strong",
and "Spiritual Kryptonite"

—

Julie Keene Ballard has inspired my life with her ability to stay constant through all of life's storms. I remember rooming with Julie at Jacobs Well and night upon night I would enter our room and find her before the Lord on her face. I watched her come face to face with things inside of herself, as she lay face down on the floor and give her whole self freely only to come up more new than the day before. In those moments, she would arise in victory, determined to fight for her God given destiny. She taught me in those moments what strength was. It wasn't that you knew it all or had it all together rather to continue to be the student and to be able to say, "I don't have it together" and to reengage after you have been defeated. My friend Julie Keene Ballard is a pillar for our generation of believers, inspiring us all, helping other women find wings to fly, all whole taking true to herself and looking beautiful. Her life is a beautiful manuscript that I have had the pleasure of having a page in.

Mere words cannot express the depths of love I have for this precious woman, Lisa Daughdrill. I will try my best to give insight straight from my heart. I recall once her telling me, "Sammie, what you have to say is important so never believe otherwise." She is a direct reflection of Abba Father's unconditional love for me. This woman wouldn't think twice about inviting you in her home, feeding you or loving you like you were her own. She is a matriarch to all the ministries she is involved in. She has taught me almost everything I know spiritually but more importantly, showed in her everyday life to seek answers from God. Lisa is one of the most humble people you would ever meet and is a laid down lover for Christ. If you know Lisa Daughdrill you love her, and if you are known by her you are loved. Beauty in its finest form, Proverbs 31 Woman.

Arise in Victory Beloved, go unto the world in love...take my eyes and my heart. See their hurt and pain? I came to demolish this from the world. Love them, be with them. Always stay mine and bring them to me...

Samantha Bang
Minister of our Lord Jesus Christ
Spreader of the Gospel
Friend

Having known Lisa for over 10 years and Julie for three, I know these two women are Overcomers in every sense of the word. They both have overcome so much in their lives with grace, mercy, and love. Although they both had unimaginable situations happen to them, they chose not to let it define them. They chose victory instead! I believe Genesis 50:20 describes it best...

Genesis 50:20 - You intended to harm me, but God intended it for good to accomplish what is now being done, the saving of many lives.

Trina Pruett Smith
Women's Ministry Leader, Counselor, Teacher
Precious Pearls Café
Pearl River, LA

I am honored to have served alongside these two warriors (Julie and Lisa as we stepped into dark places snatching men, women, and children from the pit. I remember Julie when she stepped across the threshold of Jacob's Well Ministries for Women. Her very first day there, she had only the clothes on her back. She was very frail could in no way lift her head up because she was in so much pain from the thing we call life. I watched her as a glimpse of

—

hope begin to ignite in her through the devotions given on a daily basis. I saw her go from being a victim to shouting out, "I have victory in Christ Jesus!" Her story resonates of how God will take your misery and make it your ministry. I met Mrs. Lisa, who was a devoted volunteer leading devotions at Jacob's Well Ministries for Women and I just loved her spirit. I remember one night Apostle Arthur Smith came and led devotion at Jacob's Well and the Holy Spirit spoke to me Judges 3:9 to give to Lisa.

Judges 3:9 - But when they cried out to the LORD, he raised up for them a deliverer

After devotion was over, I gave Lisa what the Holy Spirit gave me. She began to weep and said it was confirmation of what God had been speaking to her. Not long after that, Lisa and David Daughdrill open up their home to help women in transition from Jacob's Well and Grace House was born, offering a safe place for women to begin a new life instead of returning to the old life left behind. Lisa Daughdrill and Julie's life stories prove that God will take our ashes and turn them into beauty. This book will show God's grace to do for us what we can't do for ourselves. The greater the trial, the greater the blessings! It's the things we go through that makes us who we are. Today, Lisa and Julie can say "It Was Necessary" to go from pain to purpose or from victim to victory.

Elder Minister Joann Graham, Trinity Outreach Ministries
Lieutenant, Pearl River County Sheriff's Department
Picayune, MS

CONTENTS

Julie's Prologue

So begins my story. This is the beginning of the grieving process which is the end of satan's hold; therefore, this is the beginning of God's FULL inhabitance of <u>all</u> my being. See, the end of something is always the beginning of something else.

Ecclesiastes 7:8 (NIV) - The end of a matter is better than its beginning, and patience is better than pride.

This is the closing of one chapter, possibly even an entire book, only to open to a fresh new page with a new story and a new adventure. God had written down my story long before I was ever created, so I ponder the questions I am so used to asking when He already knew how this entire tale would play out.

Psalm 139:13-16 (NIV) - For you created my innermost being; you knit me together in my mother's womb. I praise you because I am fearfully and wonderfully made; your works are wonderful, I know that full well. My frame was not hidden from you when I was made in the secret place, when I was woven together in the depths of the earth. Your eyes saw my unformed body; all the days ordained for me were written in your book before one of them came to be.

He knew exactly when, where, why, how, and what for. All that was left for me to do was walk it out. I walked alright. I was an Israelite, roaming through the wilderness, complaining, angry, hopeless. I wandered around with knowledge of God but never letting Him in, not all the way. I worried too much, I grumbled about every provision, and I went from chapter to chapter in the same sad book day after day.

The adventure intensified and the plot thickened as I allowed fear, rejection, abandonment, self-loathing, anger, denial, paranoia, doubt, insecurity, and hate to flood my soul. Those spirits came in and I welcomed them right into my story and for a moment I was denied access to the Promised Land, but only for a season. I became so rigid in my views of life that I lost my sensitivity to the true reason for being good, which is to honor God. The good news is that I didn't die in the wilderness, even though I deserved death. Jesus Christ came to this wretched earth to die for me so that I could wake up every morning with new mercy.

Lamentations 3:22-23 (NIV) - Because of the LORD's great love we are not consumed, for his compassions never fail. They are new every morning; great is your faithfulness.

Grief, or the lack thereof in my case, has kept me wandering the wilderness and growing weary by the minute. However, TODAY, I am ready to enter the Promised Land. In order to do that, I must at least acknowledge where I am, go back and start at Chapter One, and <u>really read</u> the story of my life. It is going to be painful, but pain is in the offering. My purpose will prevail.

The following pages outline my life…the good, the bad, and the ugly. This is my healing. This is where God is going to smash the enemy and speak truth into every situation that brought me sadness and despair. This is where hope will rise and a new book can begin. I'm throwing everything into the wind and there will come new meaning to everything done under the sun.

"Hi, my name is Julie and I am an addict." That is how I used to introduce myself at Anonymous Meetings when I was there seeking a "Higher Power" to save me from myself. I didn't even know what to believe in other than the lies the enemy told me. I idolized all the wrong things and ended up making excuse after excuse in order to continue to check out of my self-inflicted, painful life that was created out of my own victimization, guilt, shame, remorse, and FEAR.

2 Timothy 1:7 - For the Spirit God gave us does not make us timid, but gives us power, love and self-discipline.

I suffered from addiction for over 20 years. After the suicide of my father in 1992, I went on a bender that seemed would never end. Somehow I was able to graduate from high school and college, work, get married, have children, and survive, all while suffering in silence and harming everyone who loved me and cared for me. I was lost, I was broken, my marriage ended, I lost custody of my children, and I tried to end it all. Life as I knew it was a living hell. I was playing roles every moment of every day. I can say I tried, but to me trying means being inactive and complaining about it. I did a lot of that. I moved states, recovery centers, detox centers, anonymous rooms, churches, and another broken marriage....all searching for truth. I took on two personalities, one that helped me survive in the ghetto when I was trying to score, and one that I had to survive the work force and the demands of being a wife and mother, both for which I was completely unprepared. I was addicted to MORE, to everything, to anything. My addiction took me places I never belonged, designer drugs were traded for hard core street drugs when the high was no longer satisfying my desire to run from myself and the depression that wracked my entire spiritual being, it cost me more than I could pay, and kept me longer than I wanted to stay. I was stuck and saw no way out, so I used that as an excuse to stay checked out of life as well. Hindsight is 20/20 and looking back I can clearly see the lies that entered my spirit long before I ever took the first drug or ingested the first drink. Excuses are the bricks that build a house of failure and I was full of them. More was never enough. I was putty in the hands of the enemy.

My addiction was triggered by my inability to cope with life in general. I had a desire to feel accepted from a very young age. My dad had gone to prison when I was in the 5th grade and needless to say, my entire life as I knew it was thrown up into the air and landed back on the ground not even resembling the way it was before. It was a nightmare of epic proportions in the mind of an intuitive adolescent girl who thrived in controlled environments. The spirits of rejection and abandonment took over my life and my being. The thing is I realize now that life is all about choices. Was I able to make choices about my future at such a young age? No. Was I able to grasp the reality of what was taking place in the peripherals? Absolutely not. Was I able to truly handle the deceit of the person I trusted the most? No way. However, I was able to make decisions as I grew older, and I feel like "triggers" are just another pretext used to check out of life. I made my own choices. I stepped in my own holes. There is no real justification for why I chose a path of self-destruction, other than I just did. To place blame on ANYTHING would be completely unfair. I stood there for the majority of my adult life, blame-thrower in hand, ready to fire. I triggered myself.

I moved from Virginia to Mississippi after a horrible relapse and another stay at another treatment center where I knew all the answers in order to get by and get out, quickly. I did what I always did best and separated my head from my heart and ran. I ran away from responsibility again and justified every single step that I took that would get me further away from the truth of who I was. Geographical cures do not work because the enemy is always waiting at the front door of every new location, unless you are carrying Jesus with you, and I wasn't. I found myself on the street again, living in abandoned houses or sheds, giving myself away, piece by piece, in order to get the next high. There was a street in Meridian, MS that I called home and every day as I walked my beat I passed an abandoned house on Royal Road that seemed like the perfect location to get away, to use my drug of choice without interruption, to sleep when able. However, every time I passed that house and went to step foot on the property, I was pushed back by some unseen force that wasn't familiar to me. I would like to call it "fear", but it was much deeper than that, the feeling that I got each time I went to defile that old house. I pondered it time and again as I walked, watching it from the other side of the street. I left the streets, checked into rehab number 10, and tried again to find hope in a "Higher Power" in anonymous rooms.

I left Meridian and traded those streets for the horrific ghetto of Hattiesburg, MS. I died on the street in Hattiesburg after several vain attempts to secure myself a bed at a place called Jacob's Well Recovery Center for Women. I was penniless, hopeless, and completely lost. I had heard about Jacob's Well from a counselor at a treatment center that kicked me out because I had no insurance. I had only been there 2 days when they found out about my dire situation and sent me back out to the streets that consumed me. Several days later, as I lie on the ground in the middle of the road from an overdose, my heart slowing its beat, I lost my life as I knew it. When I found myself walking down the street again, I was overcome with fear. I truly believed I was in hell and if I were to turn around, I would see my own lifeless body lying in the road. Circumstances changed and my spiritual eyes were open to the truth from the front porch with no electricity and no running water which I called home. I walked away from that porch, from that street, and found myself the very next day walking across the doorframe of Jacob's Well, by the grace of God.

After graduation from the 6 month work and worship program, I saw a picture on Susan Haynes Brogan's (the President of Jacob's Well) Facebook page that stopped my heart yet again. It was a picture of an old abandoned house, on Royal Road in Meridian, MS. It was the house where the Holy Spirit came through the Haynes family (the founders of Jacob's Well Ministries) like a flood and their lives were changed. It is the house where their lives ended and a new life with Jesus began. It was the very same house I used to cruise by. There are no coincidences in this life. Every single step is guided by God and the way is prepared, even in the darkest moments when we see no end to our suffering and our pain. He is always with us. I became a staff member of Jacob's Well, a lifelong friend and family member to the Haynes, and a trusted servant of God Himself. I was and still am honored to work beside such amazing people who love God more than their own lives. God brings everything "full circle".

Jesus' sacrifice for me allows me to wake up every morning and do everything I can to get it right, to continue to press on even when things are tough, to see the potential in every single thing I touch. I was messed up, broken, bruised, ashamed, and fighting for my life from the streets that consumed me. I am being put back together and my broken heart is being mended.

Genesis 50:20 - You intended to harm me, but God intended it for good to accomplish what is now being done, the saving of many lives.

Today, I sit in victory over satan because of the sacrifice Jesus made for me on the cross. He died in my place so I could be set free! The battle is still raging around me, but I am safe in the storm. I came into the world free and intend to leave the same way. The Lord is using my test as a Testimony to His saving grace and I want to give a voice to those suffering in silence. He is bringing it all back around for His glory! I had to come to the realization that I am not perfect, nor will I ever be until I see Him face to face in heaven. I had to loose myself from old ways of thinking and fully surrender everything in my life to Him. Today, I hold onto promises. I hold onto truth. I hold onto hope. In the eyes of the world, I will always be an addict, I will be labeled as a terrible mother, and I will be rejected by a society that lives in shallow boxes, but God...

God says that I am fearfully and wonderfully made. He says that I am the head and not the tail. He says that He will never leave me, nor forsake me. God says that He will repay me for all the years that I have squandered, the years the locusts have eaten. He says in His awesome Word that I am worthy, I am loved, I am blessed, I am equipped for His service, and I am FREE! I was in exile. I was lost. I was captive to my own depravity and my own circumstances had me bound to the floor by chains that I put on my own limbs and attached to with locks so tight I couldn't move. Today, I seek God with all my heart and I find Him EVERYWHERE! My future is bright and I do have hope!

My desire is to see more people come to know Jesus in an intimate way. I long to see the light come on in eyes that were so veiled that brilliance no longer shone from them. I want to see people free from the bondage that so easily entangles. I have a purpose and it is to be part of the Great Commission. I am ready and I am able! I pray this book will touch you in such a mighty way. I pray that you, too, regardless of your current circumstances, can see the Truth beyond the lie and become victorious through Christ Jesus.

I had a beautiful vision one glorious day when I was meditating on the Word of God and spending time in His presence through prayer, when I saw clearly in my spiritual vision the name that God gave me when he formed me in my mother's womb and sent me to the earth for His purpose and glory. He called my name to the heavens and I was destined to live out the life that was written for me long before I came to the earth, however painful. He knew that I would survive. He knew that I would glorify Him in the end. My name, is VICTORY.

Isaiah 49:1-4 - Listen to me, O coastlands,
and give attention, you peoples from afar.
The LORD called me from the womb,
from the body of my mother He named my name.
He made my mouth like a sharp sword;
in the shadow of His hand He hid me;
He made me a polished arrow;
in His quiver He hid me away.
And He said to me, "You are my servant,
Israel, in whom I will be glorified."
But I said, "I have labored in vain;
I have spent my strength for nothing and vanity;
yet surely my right is with the LORD,
and my recompense with my God."

Psalm 139 - You have searched me, LORD,
and You know me.
You know when I sit and when I rise;
You perceive my thoughts from afar.
You discern my going out and my lying down;
You are familiar with all my ways.
Before a word is on my tongue
You, LORD, know it completely.

You hem me in behind and before,
and You lay Your hand upon me.
Such knowledge is too wonderful for me,
too lofty for me to attain.
Where can I go from Your Spirit?
Where can I flee from Your presence?
If I go up to the heavens, You are there;
if I make my bed in the depths, You are there.
If I rise on the wings of the dawn,
if I settle on the far side of the sea,
even there Your hand will guide me,
Your right hand will hold me fast.
If I say, "Surely the darkness will hide me
and the light become night around me,"
even the darkness will not be dark to You;
the night will shine like the day,
for darkness is as light to You.
For You created my inmost being;
You knit me together in my mother's womb.
I praise You because I am fearfully and wonderfully made;
Your works are wonderful,
I know that full well.
My frame was not hidden from You
when I was made in the secret place,
when I was woven together in the depths of the earth.
Your eyes saw my unformed body;
all the days ordained for me were written in Your book
before one of them came to be.
How precious to me are Your thoughts, God!
How vast is the sum of them!
Were I to count them,
they would outnumber the grains of sand —
when I awake, I am still with You.
If only You, God, would slay the wicked!
Away from me, you who are bloodthirsty!
They speak of You with evil intent;
Your adversaries misuse Your name.

—

Do I not hate those who hate You, LORD,
and abhor those who are in rebellion against You?
I have nothing but hatred for them;
I count them my enemies.
Search me, God, and know my heart;
test me and know my anxious thoughts.
See if there is any offensive way in me,
and lead me in the way everlasting.

I am honored to collaborate with the co-author of this book, a woman after God's own heart. Her story, too, is one of pure redemption through Christ Jesus. Her God given knowledge of the scriptures that lead us through the process of grief is a gift directly from heaven. She has counseled hundreds and hundreds of souls that hunger to be free from the bondage of grief and sadness, and she does so out of her very own pain and experience. God never takes us through things unless He is to get all the glory, honor, and praise, and Lisa Daughdrill is a prime example of taking something that was meant for harm and turning it into life lessons for everyone to benefit from and grow closer to Christ through.

Lisa's Prologue

Victory - Suffering that brings praise, honor and glory to Christ.

Psalms 31:19 - How great is Your goodness, which You have stored up for those who fear You, which You have wrought for those who take refuge in You, before the sons of men!

Hey Y'all. My name is Lisa. Unlike my sophisticated co-author, I am a seasoned country lady from Mississippi with a fair amount of silver in my crown of glory, so you will find my writing style to be a bit different, but both of us are Holy Spirit led in this book. It's our hope that in sharing here from our hearts and lives, that you too will grasp hold of the healing and freedom that we have been given, and the Truth that we so desperately want to pass on to others.

I have been called here by the Lord to share with you the hope, joy, peace and abundant life that I and countless others have found in Christ no matter what situations or circumstances come against us. I call it the secret to truly living the abundant life.

Ephesians 3:20-21 - Now to Him who is able to do far more abundantly beyond all that we ask or think, according to the power that works within us, to Him be the glory in the church and in Christ Jesus to all generations forever and ever. Amen

God actually told me in 2009 that I would be writing two books with "Julie", I just didn't know until recently that He meant THIS Julie as a writing partner. You see, I have a life-long friend also named Julie, who at that time in 2009 was spiritually mentoring me and encouraging me to journal. In fact, I wrote a 150 page journal account of my testimony centered on the relationship God had formed between my childhood friend Julie and me, her family, and the resulting relationship with Christ I found through them. It was during the journaling that God began the painful healing process of my facing and overcoming the unresolved grief I had suffered from for a period of 32 years. I naturally assumed she was the Julie that the Lord was telling me that I would write with.

Now, mind you, that when God spoke to me about two books I'd write with Julie, this was many years prior to my meeting the co-author of this book, Ms. Julie Keene. Therefore, I mistakenly assumed what God meant, looking for opportunities in the wrong place, and getting discouraged by the other Julie's lack of enthusiasm in our doing joint book projects. I knew what God had told me, but rather than just wait until He clarified or told me the next step of His plan, and showed me exactly who it actually involved, I jumped in like Sari with Hagar and tried to do it for Him in my own will, way and time. After a while as I grew in the Lord, I learned to let go of that infant's eagerness to get ahead of God and realized in my own strength it was a waste of time causing me much <u>frustration - when expectation and reality collide.</u>

Well here we are, years later, in God's perfect, patient, all-knowing time, writing with THE Julie on THE book that HE intended. I'm so thankful our Creator is so much smarter and better at planning my life than I am – Thank You Lord!

Job 37:5 - God thunders with His voice wondrously, doing great things which we cannot comprehend.

Isaiah 55:8-9 - For My thoughts are not your thoughts, Nor are your ways My ways, declares the Lord. For as the heavens are higher than the earth, so are My ways higher than your ways and My thoughts than your thoughts.

My purpose in this writing is to shed Light on the dark areas of grief and hopefully show you that grief can be used for good, yes I said good, as the catalyst to draw you and others closer in relationship with God and to change your life for the better, as well as all the other people who see and hear you as you walk out your journey glorifying God.

When I began teaching and counseling on grief, the name God gave me for the ministry work is Good Grief. You see, grief in itself is not always dark and bad. Yes, it hurts, but it does not have to consume or destroy us. We don't have to get bitter. We can use it to good, ours and others, while we are getting better.

I've heard many times that God doesn't call the equipped, He equips those He calls. I guess I'm proof of that too. Sharing the gospel of Jesus Christ is my calling and teaching others how they too can be free from all bondage is my ministry. A big part of that ministry centers on Grief recovery, addiction recovery, and overcoming all the behaviors that go along with them. My mission is to expose the devil for the liar he is and to share the Truth of God's Word, His Promises, and how to apply the Word and the promises in our everyday life in order to live the abundant life in Christ that I and so many others have found.

To give you a glimpse of my qualifications, and as living proof that there is Good Grief – turning our worst pain into our greatest joy, I'll give a little of my own testimony. The reason I know these things I'm sharing is because I have experienced grief both ways – bitter and better. Trust me, Better is Better.

As a young girl and teen I had many traumatic experiences in my life; rape, teen pregnancy, abortion, and then in 1978, as a 17 year old, the love of my young life, the man that I had planned to spend my life with, suddenly fell to his death in a work accident one day. I did not know anything about grief or that the things I was feeling were common stages of grief, all compounded from one unresolved traumatic event to the next. With this loss being the final blow in my heart and mind, I certainly didn't know how to begin to recover from this thing that consumed me. I didn't yet understand that it was an emotional condition I was in that had a process to its end, and it was called grief.

I didn't talk to my family or anyone else about how I felt for fear that I was going crazy because I couldn't control the way I felt or the things that went through my mind anymore and would act out of those uncontrolled feelings. Running, denial, and justification became my mode of operation and I learned you could fool anyone if you kept a smile plastered on your face. I was afraid if I spoke what I really felt and believed, it would all be out in the open and others would find out I was crazy and maybe even commit me or something. I believed that I was so sinful from the things of my past that God had taken the only person who ever truly loved me.

satan stepped right in to twist and turn the truth in so many ways, constantly reminding me how hopeless my life was each time I tried to get up. I would self-sabotage any good things in my life, believing the lie that I didn't deserve them or that they would realize the "truth – satan's lies" about me and it would all be over anyways. The enemy really made my head spin as he was opening all the doors I needed to lead me right on to self-destruction. I started experiencing severe depression and I began to sleep a lot, even as a high school senior, and used alcohol regularly to try to numb all the pain, shame, and guilt. But then there were actions and consequences of my drinking, so the pain, shame, and guilt came back full circle requiring more chemical numbing. Soon, other addictive behaviors began to manifest themselves in those times when I didn't drink. This silent hell of binge drinking, compulsive shopping, compulsive eating, and yes, even compulsive religious practices, went on for years.

I did not have a personal relationship with Jesus at that time. I thought I did, growing up in Church, asking Jesus to come into my heart to save me and being Baptized at 9 years old, but it was many years later after I had nearly destroyed my life and caused great pain to myself and everyone who had ever loved me, that I found out differently. The only relationship we had was me running in self-will and then begging for help when the consequences came and promising I'd never be bad again if He did. I wasn't mentally ill, I was spiritually ill. I was living in deception and unresolved grief, apart from God. That's a bitter place to find yourself.

As time went on, I also had more grief in my life that continued the compounding effects following divorce and financial loss, a total change of my life and my children's lives, continually feeling like a failure, drinking in self-pity, asking why I couldn't seem to succeed, and then wondering at 29 years old with a minimum wage job, struggling, raising two children alone, if this was all there was to life. Oh my goodness how blind I was not to see all the bountiful blessings I had, but instead I focused on what I didn't have that I thought I wanted.

—

There in the midst of the painful journey, in 1992, I finally came to the end of myself and saw my need for a real savior other than myself. It was then that God stepped in through an intervention by my long-time friend Darleen, who recognized my addiction and in unconditional love took immediate action. When I surrendered the battle, God then truly saved me, delivering my soul from hell and my life from the hell of addiction and all the destruction that comes with it. By the Grace of God I was set free on January 26, 1992.

If you don't see anything else here, please see that my friend's one selfless act of confronting the lie of my addiction head on, and speaking Truth to me in the face of the lie I was living, not only helped me and my family, but has had a ripple effect over all these many years, touching untold numbers of others as I continue to reach out to others in need and they go on to do the same. One person can make a difference. I was saved and transformed, clean and sober, but the Lord and I still had some unfinished business on my hidden, unresolved grief that I carried deep down under the surface in my heart for another 17 years.

It was in 2009 when I came to a place that I began questioning and seeking more in my relationship with God, asking God to give me more understanding of Who He is and how I fit into His picture, asking God for more closeness in our communication and to experience more of His Presence, that He told me very clearly, but gently and mercifully, that it was time for us to first address that long hidden pain that I still secretly carried and had refused to lay down and bury. It had been festering like a deep splinter in my heart, a bitter pill that I swallowed and didn't even realize I had allowed it to cloud every relationship I had ever had and even become a barrier between me and God for all those years.

I had made the loss and grief my idol without ever even recognizing it. It had also robbed me from experiencing the fullness of joy, my joy of the Lord and my joy of life. That prayerful conversation that day began a two year journey where I learned all about grief –taught by the Master, a lesson that not only completely healed me of unresolved grief in all those areas that I had carried all my life, but prepared me to go ye therefore and teach others as the Holy Spirit led me in the Name of the Father, and the Son, and the Holy Spirit. It brought me closer to God than I had ever been. It gave great purpose to my pain, opened my heart and my eyes to a full relationship with God and so therefore became "good" grief. I was on the mountaintop.

Then right at that time when I had just finished the last chapter or so I thought, of the end of the testimony book on my grief recovery journey, on May 14, 2011, my beloved 22 year old son, Jordan Daniel Byrd (Jordi), suddenly died of a methadone drug overdose on the couch in our living room one night. Jordi was a Christian, a college student who had struggled with addiction but gotten clean and dedicated his life to serve God in ministry in the months prior to his death. To say my mountain shook is an understatement. I loved my son more than life itself. BUT GOD! My merciful Lord prepared the way for me and has carried me every step in this journey and has never let me down. His grace truly is sufficient.

Deuteronomy 31:8 - The Lord is the one who goes ahead of you; He will be with you. He will not fail you or forsake you. Do not fear or be dismayed.

This time I knew exactly what grief was and I was not going to let it destroy me. I knew who the enemy was that had brought this destructive attack on me and my family and I vowed that very day I would NOT allow satan any glory in my son's life or death! I would praise my God in the midst of the storm and I would use my son's death as a testimony to God's saving grace glory.

Because of the agony I had lived through before, I knew the dangers of going through grief apart from God, how easily satan can use it to overtake us if we don't press through the stages of recovery with our focus on Christ, and how painful it is if we don't draw on the Comfort of the Holy Spirit. I also knew this time I must immediately call out to my God for help and refuge and fix my eyes firmly on Jesus to ensure that I could walk on these storm tossed waters, and not sink. I still had my first-born son, Justin, who was also grieving the loss of his little brother, and I knew Justin needed me to be a strong testimony to the Grace, Comfort & Peace of Jesus to him. I also had a wonderful godly husband who loved me so selflessly and I knew that he didn't deserve to lose his wife just because of the tragedy our family had suffered. It would have been so easy to selfishly stop living in the name of grief, but my family didn't deserve to lose me too. No, I would live life abundantly as a testimony to God and as an honor to Jordi who would have never wanted me to hurt or stop living because of him. To do so would have been an insult to who my son was and the love he had for others.

2 Timothy 3:14-15 - You, however, continue in the things you have learned and become convinced of, knowing from whom you have learned them, and that from childhood you have known the sacred writings which are able to give you the wisdom that leads to salvation through faith which is in Christ Jesus.

Out of the ashes of my son's death, God used it to strengthen my faith, witness to others, step out of my traditional woman's-place in ministry upbringing and answer His call that His sons and daughters would prophesy, sending me forth as an anointed Woman of God to Evangelize, preaching and teaching the Gospel of Jesus Christ wherever He sent me. God used Jordi's death to push me out of my boxed in comfort zone and into His destiny purpose for me.

In the summer of 2012, after looking for a Christ centered grief recovery group in my area and finding none, God opened the door for me to begin Good Grief Ministries. Through that first group, Jesus Christ brought hope and healing and even salvation to many. He has provided me with many speaking opportunities to testify far and wide, teaching and preaching. In 2013 He led my husband and me to open our personal home as a safe-house transitional home called Grace House, an in-house 6 month discipleship/second phase recovery program for women who have graduated Jacob's Well Recovery Center. Within the first 3 years the Lord brought 25 women and several of their children through our home and we are thankful to have been used in that part of their journeys. I also lead devotions at Jacob's Well and at their men's recovery center, Damascus Road, and do grief counseling with the women and men of the two recovery programs, as well as offering after care and private counseling at Grace House for others. It was through our ministry work with Jacob's Well that I was greatly blessed to meet and come to love my dear friend, Julie Keene. In addition to the work we do with the two recovery centers, my husband David and I also do volunteer work with other local ministries, churches and Christian organizations, as well as serving in the mission field with a National Christian Disaster Relief organization, and also as a part of a ministry team to Native Americans.

Recently, as I concluded a Sunday morning sermon as a guest Pastor filling a partner-ministry's pulpit, an older gentleman, unknown to me, approached patiently waiting as others came and went by to bid me well. At first I thought he may be waiting for another person but as I saw him from the corner of my eye continue to stand in wait and then following me out, down the hallway past the fellowship hall of gathering people toward the exit door, I could tell he must seriously desire to speak with me. As I stopped, he smiled and quietly, almost shyly said, "Holy Spirit told me to tell you something." Well of course as a woman stepping down from a pulpit in South Mississippi, you just never know what that could mean, but he looked sincere and harmless enough so I said "yes, please tell me." Then he, not knowing anything about me, leaned in near my ear and delivered the most beautiful message to me. He said "He wants you to know that adversity is a gift that God gives to His closest friends", and he stepped back and smiled so sweetly as if savoring the job that he had just completed. Mind you, this man and I had never met and I'm pretty sure he knew nothing of my testimony or grief history.

I thought about that as I drove home that day as I have many days since, realizing how very true that is. My God is so loving and merciful. He has allowed many heartaches and adversities in this life to come my way, not to destroy me, no never meaning to destroy because that's not Who God is, but all were meant to send me running back to Him, my Creator, into His loving, compassionate arms, to draw me ever closer in relationship with Him.

It has been in those times of painful loss, when my world as I knew it had been shaken - the two year bedridden illness of my Daddy, his death in 2008, my son's battle with addiction and his overdose death in 2011, and the sudden death of my big sister in 2014 – that I have come to know personally the compassionate working of Grace and Who the Comforter really is.

—

It was also through my seeking the Lord in pain that He has done amazing transforming work on me continually preparing me and teaching me how to let go of the things of this world while looking through the glass at the eternal picture, ever moving forward without fear to my eternal home with Him. He is my closest friend.

Romans 8:28 - And we know that God causes all things to work together for good to those who love God, to those who are called according to His purpose.

Intertwined here with Julie Keene's beautifully articulated testimony, is my attempt to explain to those who, like me, did not know what grief really consists of or that any traumatic or life changing event or circumstance can cause grief, not just the death of a loved one. I want you to see that there are stages of the grief recovery process and it is a process. All people go through these stages to varying degrees, at varying times, some immediate, some delayed reactions, and stay in one or more stages for varying lengths of time. The grieving process can be as individual as the person but it's when we don't grieve or don't move through them and get stuck in the process, that the destructive power of unresolved grief sets in and sucks the life out of us as well as those around us who love us.

The 7 Common Stages of Grief are:

1) Shock & Denial
2) Pain & Guilt
3) Anger & Bargaining
4) Depression, Reflection, & Loneliness
5) The Upward Turn
6) Reconstruction & Working Through
7) Acceptance & Hope.

—

I will explain more about these 7 common stages of grief as we take a closer look at them through Julie's testimony.

So what is grief?

Grief, as defined in the Holman Bible Dictionary, are practices and emotions associated with the experience of the death of a loved one or of another catastrophe or tragedy. Some common causes of grief: death of loved one, divorce or relationship breach, violence perpetrated against you or a loved one, violence witnessed against another person, loss of virginity for an unmarried woman or man whether rape or consensual, loss of career/job, loss of health for yourself or a loved one, loss of financial security or loss of anything you deem a personal security or threat thereto, the after effects of natural or manmade disasters such as hurricane, tornado, terrorist attack, etc., and after effect of unrepentant sin, willful disobedience to God.

Grief can come from any life changing event. Since death is a part of life and no one escapes it, grief and mourning are mentioned quite often in the Bible. It is a natural way for us to deal with disappointments, losses and major changes in our lives. The Bible tells us that Jesus wept and that the Holy Spirit is grieved by our unholy actions.
When death is mentioned in the Bible, frequently it relates to the experience of the bereaved, who always responded immediately, outwardly, and without reserve, unlike many of us who believe it is a sign of weakness to cry or show emotion. Many times the mourner tore his clothes, smeared ashes on his forehead and put on sackcloth, a dark material made from camel or goat hair and used for making grain bags. The women usually put on black clothing and covered their heads as a sign of mourning.

The mourner often walked barefoot, wept often and loudly for others to see, and the men often cut their hair, and beard, even cutting their skin disfiguring the body. Fasting was sometimes involved, usually only during the day typically for seven days and friends brought meals in since food could not be prepared in a house rendered unclean by the presence of the dead. Not only did the actual relatives mourn, but they might hire professional mourners as well.

Through this book it is my hope that you can learn how to dispel the all-too-common lies that satan uses in order to keep us bound regardless of your circumstance, but especially in the torrential waves of emotion that comes with grief.

For those of you who are avid proof-readers, you will have to give me a little mercy here because I intentionally do not ever capitalize the name satan. I don't want to give him any credence where possible. This lower case snub is done out of my total disgust for him, however in my adoration for My Lord, The Holy Trinity of God, I always capitalize God, Jesus, Holy Spirit, and He, Him and Them when referring to any or all of Them. It's just one of my little quirks.

I hope that if you don't know already that one of the things you will see in this book is that satan as well as all his demonic spirit army are our real enemy; they have one purpose and that is to steal, kill, and destroy me, Julie, you, and all other humans. But Christ is our Friend and Savior, The One and Only who came to give us abundant life. By the Grace of God and the blood shedding sacrifice of Jesus Christ and His resurrected life, Julie and I are both the children today of the Most High King, joint heirs with Jesus in the family of God. It's through our seeking Christ and making Him first in our lives, studying God's Word

—

and applying those principles and Truths to our lives, that the dirty dog devil has no hold on us any longer.

Philippians 4:13 - I can do all things through Him (Christ) who strengthens me.

You too have this freedom within you if you know Jesus Christ as your personal Savior and have the power of the Comforter, The Holy Spirit within you to overcome anything, if you allow Him to be Lord over your life. If not yet, then I pray that by the end of this book you see your need for a Savior other than yourself or another human, both being incapable, and you cry out humbly to Jesus for His Saving Grace (He doing for us what we cannot do for ourselves). He is faithful to save.

John 15:13 - Greater love has no one than this, that one lay down his life for his friends.

John 3:16-17 - For God so loved the world, that He gave His only begotten Son, that whoever believes in Him shall not perish, but have eternal life. For God did not send the Son into the world to judge the world, but that the world might be saved through Him.

I don't know about you, but the enemy has stolen enough from me in my past until I came to understand what the battle is and how to overcome the daily attacks, securely knowing that the overall Victory has already been won for me. Sadly, before I became enlightened to these facts, I had unknowingly given away to the enemy many of life's greatest blessings through my lack of godly wisdom, pride, fear, and most assuredly, unresolved grief, without ever realizing I didn't have to. In my past, I actually made it easy for him to steal my blessings - spiritual, mental, relational, and physical, nearly destroying me and others in the process. But today, I know who I am as a Child of God and I refuse to allow the enemy any glory in anything in my life. Today it is my greatest desire to share these same principles and truths, the tools that I have learned to use with others to spread hope found only in Christ.

1 John 5:4 - For whatever is born of God overcomes the world; and this is the victory that has overcome the world – our faith.

God Loves you and I Love you, Keep walking.

More on Lies vs Truth

Your Strategic Weapon: Truth – we must know better in order to do better!

First, in order to counter a lie, there are a few things we must learn to identify, believe and do.

I.   We must know Truth to be able to recognize a lie.

There is only one source for the infallible Truth and that is God. Truth must always line up with God's Word or it is not Truth. In the Bible "truth" is not an abstract ideal or philosophical concept. The Hebrew and Greek words for "truth" share a common meaning that a thing is "true" when it corresponds to reality. All that the Scriptures in both Old and New Testaments teach is in the fullest harmony with reality.

Jesus Christ is The Way, <u>The Truth</u> and the Life; no one comes to the Father but through Him. - John 14:6

Truth will set you free. - John 8:32

God is Light. In Him there is no darkness at all. - 1 John 1:5

It is impossible for God to lie. - Hebrews 6:18; Numbers 23:19; Titus 1:2; 1 Samuel 15:29; Psalms 92:15; Malachi 3:6; Romans 3:4

II.   We must understand who the source of the lie is.

satan is the father of all lies. - John 8:44; John 3:20-21

The Holman Bible Dictionary defines the name satan as the transliteration of the Hebrew word meaning *adversary*, normally translated in English as *adversary or accuser*.

Wow, there's our source right there, again that dirty dog devil, no matter whose mouth he uses to speak the lie from. We know this to be true because God told us in John 8:44 that *satan is the father of all lies*. Just as God is the one source for Truth, there is also only one source for all lies and that is satan. So now we know who the source of the lie we are hearing is.

If you still aren't convinced that the devil is your enemy, or that he is the one leading and using others to battle against you, let me list here just a few of the many other names that the Bible uses for him to give a clearer picture of his sinister character.

abaddon – Hebrew name for satan meaning destruction. - Revelation 9:11
accuser – Revelation 12:10
adversary and roaring lion – 1 Peter 5:8
angel of light – 2 Corinthians 11:14-15 ("No wonder, for even satan disguises himself as an angel of light, therefore it is not surprising if his servants also disguise themselves as servants of righteousness, whose end will be according to their deeds")
apollyon – Greek name for satan meaning destroyer. - Revelation 9:11
beelzebub – the ruler of the demons. - Matthew 12:24
deceiver – Revelation 12:9
enemy – Matthew 13:39
evil one – John 17:15
god of this age – 2 Corinthians 4:4 ("Whose minds the god of this age has blinded, who do not believe, lest the light of the gospel of the glory of Christ, who is the image of God, should shine on them")

lawless one – 2 Thessalonians 2:8-10
liar and murderer – John 8:44
rulers of the darkness – Ephesians 6:12 ("For we do not wrestle against flesh and blood, but against principalities, against powers, against the rulers of the darkness of this age, against spiritual hosts of wickedness in the heavenly places"
tempter – Matthew 4:3
thief – John 10:10
wicked one – Ephesians 6:16

But, take heart friend, because the Truth of God's Word in 1 John 4:4-6 says, "_You are from God, little children, and have overcome them; because greater is He who is in you than he who is in the world. They are from the world; therefore they speak as from the world, and the world listens to them. We are from God; he who knows God listens to us; he who is not from God does not listen to us. By this we know the spirit of truth and the spirit of error._" AMEN!

III. We must recognize what the intent is for the lie.

satan came to steal, kill & destroy. - John 10:10

You may be asking, "WHY?" Why is satan out to get us, what did we ever do to him?? Well, basically he's just mad at God, Jesus, The Holy Spirit and all that God created, especially humans, who were created in God's image. But, here's a little explanation based on scriptural fact from Ezekiel 28:6;12-17; Isaiah 14:12-14 and the book of Revelations, as to why it is that we are in this battle of good vs evil and what caused it all in the first place even before the fall of man in the garden.

lucifer was satan's name when he was created by God at some point, we only know it was prior to the

Garden of Eden. lucifer was a beautiful angel of the highest position in heaven. He was above all the other angels as the chief covering angel who worked in the throne room of God. He was also the most beautiful of all God's angels. He was created for God's enjoyment, so that God's glory would shine through lucifer.

Ezekiel 28:12-17 describes when the light of God hit lucifer's emerald, jasper and diamonds, it would make a beautiful rainbow and magnify God's beauty, and how pipes were built in him when God's wind passed through a beautiful symphony would be heard. But then lucifer became filled with pride, wanted all glory for himself and to take over in Heaven as a god. Over time he had many other angels worshipping him instead of Jesus. lucifer refused to give up his pride so as Isaiah 14:12-14 tells us, God threw him out of Heaven, along with the angels who chose to follow him. They are demons who live in the spirit world, but they tempt and influence people here on earth.

Think about it, once the light display and sound of music were gone when lucifer was cast out, it must have been kind of void and lonely for God. But then as we know in Genesis 1:26, God created us humans out of His desire to fellowship with someone who loves Him just for Him, the same desire that we humans have, to love and be loved. God created us for fellowship with Him and to worship Him from a heart of love for Him, and to bear witness to others of His light in this otherwise dark world. If we are really a child of God, we will worship Him out of our hearts desire to fill His longing for our love; to give God affection and Praise.

satan is a prideful, bitter, angry, jealous spirit. he hates anything beautiful and righteous that glorifies God (oh my, I know some people like that too). And, since we

—

humans took his place with God in fellowship, love, and worship of God, he especially hates and wants to discredit and destroy us. he goes to great lengths and gets great pleasure in stealing our joy, confidence, and hope, because he knows if he can steal those, then he has destroyed the person. When we entertain the seed of doubt, we allow satan to impregnate our minds with negativity, where in due time we are growing and birthing our own destruction. That's how serious this stinking thinking is. We must kill it with Truth at first sign.

I want to encourage you to go on and read the end of his story though in Revelations 20. Hell was never intended for humans. It was created for the punishment of satan and his demons. However, like lucifer, we humans also have a sinful heart, except we be born again. We were born into inequity through the fall of Adam and many of us refuse to see ourselves for what we really are. We allow our self-pride and willful disobedience to God to send us to hell too, that place of unquenchable fire, weeping and gnashing of teeth - except for the Saving Grace of God through the blood purchase price paid for us by the Perfect One, Jesus. Unlike satan and his demons, we humans still have a choice while here on earth. It's not God's will that any should perish (2 Peter 3:9) but that all should come to repentance to enjoy eternal life. We can surrender our self-will at the Cross. We can turn from our prideful heart, by repenting unto salvation through Jesus Christ and then follow Him as Lord of our life.

Knowing the Intent of the Lie:

So what is a lie and what is its intention? Webster's Intermediate Dictionary tells us that a lie is:

1. To make an untrue statement with intent to deceive.

2. To create a false impression.

Look at that: the untrue statement (lie) has _the intent to deceive_ and _create a false impression_. No one even has to blatantly speak false words to us for a lie to take hold. A lie's seed can be planted in our mind simply by hearing or seeing something that gives us the impression of an untrue statement. It can be something seemingly harmless, a joke even, such as Julie testified to, a child being told one thing and her hearing and believing it to mean something totally different. There is the power of life and death in the tongue. There are so many scriptures that warn us of the dangers of an unbridled tongue. We must be careful in what we speak.

Proverbs 18:21 - Death and Life are in the power of the tongue.

James 3:5 - So also the tongue is a small part of the body, and yet it boasts of great things. See how great a forest is set aflame by such a small fire!

Proverbs 11:9 - With his mouth the godless man destroys his neighbor, but through knowledge the righteous will be delivered.

Ephesians 4:29 - Let no unwholesome word proceed from your mouth, but only such a word as is good for edification according to the need of the moment, so that it will give grace to those who hear.

The Discerning Spirit of God:

As in the example of Julie and myself, even if the lies are not audible, many times we still hear voices in our mind, some planting seeds of negativity, fear, doubt, jealously and insecurities of all kinds. No matter how subtle these voices are, we have the ability within us to distinctly hear three very separate messengers: God's

—

voice, our own thoughts, and the adversary's lies. Because most of the time they all three use our vocabulary and speech patterns, we get confused as to who we are hearing and without specific Light or practice, we can't discern the difference in the three. That's another reason we should stay in tune to the Holy Spirit within us. It is He who gives us the discerning ability to know His voice from our own or the enemy's. He will expose the flaws of our thinking as well as the enemy's lies. He will lead us in all Truth and bring the Truth of God's Word to life for our situation at any given time if we cultivate a relationship with Him and if we truly seek to know the Truth. We must be ready and willing for Him to do some heart exposure on us too in the process, to make our heart, life and will line up more with His.

2 Corinthians 10:5 – We are destroying speculations and every lofty thing raised up against the knowledge of God, and we are taking every thought captive to the obedience of Christ.

Psalms 51:6 – Behold, You desire truth in the innermost being, and in the hidden part You will make me know wisdom.

IV. We must speak Truth to ourselves with gratitude and praise for God.

Romans 10:17 - Faith comes by hearing, and hearing by the Word of God.

We must not only speak Truth to ourselves, but we must speak it over ourselves and believe it. Speak it out loud and as often as needed, which for most of us short memory human beings is multiple times daily, along with audible praise to God for His Truth, and thanking God for all His promises found in His Word in order to kill the seed of the lie, silence the enemy from our mind, send him fleeing from our presence and overcome in victory.

Praise is always an appropriate response to the power of Our Redeemer. (Remember, victory is suffering that brings praise, honor and glory to Christ). Also, Praise calls down God's very Presence! Praise is like a big special God magnet that draws Him right to us. God inhabits the praises of His people.

Psalm 22:3 - But thou art holy, O thou that inhabits the praises of Israel.

Some things to remember about Truth and Victory:

Truth shines light on darkness. Light always exposes lies. Jesus is the Light of the Earth. Our victory is found by turning our focus on Jesus no matter how dark the situation is and He will expose the lies and the liar to set your mind right in Truth.

Ephesians 4:23-25 - And that you be renewed in the spirit of your mind, and put on the new self, which in the likeness of God has been created in righteousness and holiness of the truth. Therefore, laying aside falsehood, speak truth each one of you with his neighbor, for we are members of one another.

So, now that we know who – satan; we know why – to steal, kill, and destroy; and we know what the intent is – to deceive and create a false impression, it's time for us to address the various stages of grief while we speak Truth, Life & Freedom into these lies that Julie faced chapter by chapter. While reading her story, you too can begin to speak Truth into your own life and the lies you may have heard. To derail the lie we must ALWAYS go back to the scriptures found in the Holy Bible, remembering that it is God's infallible, living, breathing Word, and listen to the Holy Spirit, who will guide and teach us in all Truth.

—

I'm going to give you a tip here, get yourself a "Bible Promise Book" to keep with you. They are small inexpensive pocket sized books that have scriptures listed by topic for easy reference such as depression, anger, fear, anxiety, rejection, etc. At any time, in any place, you can whip that little book out and go to claiming your own victory. Amen!

John 16:13 - When the Spirit of Truth comes, He will guide you into all Truth.

In Matthew 4 we find that Jesus was led up by the Spirit into the wilderness to be tempted by the devil. Amazing isn't it? That Emmanuel, God with us, Jesus, would have to go through a trying and testing period too in order to prepare Him, equip Him to be able to fulfill His destiny purpose here on earth. And just like the devil always does, he came in for the attack after Jesus had fasted 40 days and was physically and emotionally weakened. He tried to tempt Jesus with three things that he always tries to tempt us with too:

1) The Lust of the Eye
2) The Lust of the Flesh
3) The Pride of Life.

Jesus didn't argue with satan. He simply said "it is written" and quoted God's Word, rebuking the devil with the Truth. When Jesus stood on the Truth of the Word of God, it tells us in verse 11 "Then the devil left Him; and behold, angels came to minister to Him". Did you know that you can do the same thing? Rebuke the devil with the Word of God. Quote it out loud for him to hear. It's like nails running down a chalk board to the enemy. He will leave your presence until he thinks he can find another opportune time to attack again when your defenses are down.

Just like with Jesus, when we stand in battle against the enemy, and when we are worn and weary, Hebrews 1:14 tells us that God sends ministering angels to come to us too.

2 Timothy 3:16-17 - All Scripture is inspired by God and profitable for teaching, for reproof, for correction, for training in righteousness; so that the man of God may be adequate, equipped for every good work.

<u>*Chapter One*</u>

Life was normal for me as a child. I don't have a whole array of bad memories. Looking back, I remember being incredibly inquisitive. There are so many moments of quiet observation where I was merely contemplating my surroundings. Oh, I'm sure if you asked my mother, she would say I was so full of questions that I got under her skin the majority of the time, but what she doesn't realize is how many times I <u>didn't</u> ask questions. My mind was constantly in a quest to figure things out...alone.

For so many years I have wanted to remember what I wanted to remember. I forced myself to look at parts of my past through rose tinted glasses and I chose to look at some parts of my life through darkness as I groped around in the recess of my heart. Those are the parts that need revealing. That is where the Light needs to meet the dark so that healing can begin.

Ecclesiastes 7:13-14 - Consider what God has done: Who can straighten what he has made crooked? When times are good, be happy; but when times are bad, consider this: God has made the one as well as the other. Therefore, no one can discover anything about their future.

Every bad decision that was made for me, and every bad decision I made on my own, have lasting effects. Here is an example: At the Jacob's Well Thrift Stores there used to be a public restroom, until someone who wasn't thinking or in their right mind decided to leave drugs in the ceiling of the bathroom for one of the girls at the Recovery Center. No more public restrooms at Jacob's

Well Thrift Stores. It effects every elderly person, pregnant woman, small child, people with incontinence, and the women of Jacob's Well who have to continuously turn the disgruntled patrons away from the restrooms. One single decision by one uncaring, ungrateful individual has had a ripple effect on hundreds of people a week ever since, people they don't even know. That alone causes me to sit back and truly take an inventory of myself and my own selfish ways that led me to where I am today.

Philippians 2:3-4 - Do nothing out of selfish ambition or vain conceit. Rather, in humility value others above yourselves, not looking to your own interests but each of you to the interests of the others.

Negative aspects of my life caused me to make poor choices. WRONG!! I made poor choices. Period. No need for further discussion. The blame game caused me to see things distorted, like I was looking at myself and my situations through a fun house mirror.

Small, funny sayings affect small children in different ways. I never really thought about it, but rejection starts at such a young age. My dad used to joke with us and tell us that he found us in a trashcan. It was all fun and games, just his strange sense of humor pouring out. It made him laugh, so I laughed. I loved seeing my daddy in good spirits, no matter the cost. His other "joke" he used to tell me was that I was supposed to be a boy. That one didn't cause me to go "Ha-Ha" because I knew beyond a shadow of a doubt that I was the prissiest girl around.

LIE #1 – I was a mistake.

TRUTH #1 - IT IS WRITTEN: *"For You (God) formed my inward parts; You wove me in my mother's womb. I will give thanks to You, for I am fearfully and wonderfully made; Wonderful are Your works, and my soul knows it very well. My frame was not hidden from You, when I was made in secret and skillfully wrought in the depths of the earth" Psalms 139:13-15.*

No child conceived is ever a mistake to God. Julie did as most of us have done, simply mistaken her own identity as to Whose she was and why she was created.

Regardless of our earthly birth parents, whether or not they desired in their heart to have a child or put any forethought into dreaming about what that child would be like, it was out of their control anyways. We ultimately belong to God, created by Him, In Him and for Him, Colossians 1:16. We were created in His Image, Genesis 1:27 and He loves us with an everlasting love, Jeremiah 31:3

More Truth from God's Word:

You may not know who you are, but God knows everything about you. Psalm 139:1
He knew you even before you were conceived.
Jeremiah 1:4-5
He chose you when He planned creation. Ephesians 1:11-12
Even the hairs on your head are numbered.

—

Matthew 10:29-31
You were created in His Image. Genesis 1:27
He determined the exact time you would be born and where you would live. Acts 17:26
He brought you forth on the day you were born. Psalm 71:6
In God you live and move and have your being. Acts 17:28

When you look at mankind and question the good from the evil, understand that God's ways are not our ways, but yet, none were mistakes. God made all mankind in His image.

Unlike humans, Jehovah God is Sovereign, All-present, All-knowing, All-powerful, and incapable of making mistakes. So 1 Corinthians 15:9 applies to all, "I am what I am by the Grace of God".

When we study Psalms 139 we see how intricately God made each of us. He took His time and designed each of us with forethought and precision, with unique finger prints, DNA, and gifts all to be used for His glorious purposes. He says in Jeremiah 1:5 He knew us before He ever created us and Psalms 139:16 says that He knew the number of days He had for us before there was even one. That means God knew every good thing about us as well as every mistake, every sin, every fault, and every fall we would have our entire lifetime and yet He still chose to create each of us for His specific purpose anyway.

Jeremiah 29:11-13 - For I know the plans I have for you, declares the Lord, plans to prosper you and not to harm you, plans to give you hope and a future. Then you will call upon me and come and pray to me, and I will listen to you. You will seek me and find me when you seek me with all your heart.

—

Throughout the Bible we see the words God uses to tell us how special we are to Him. He chose us, He pre-destined us, He created us, He adopted us, and He grafted us into His family. Those are not words used for someone who mistakenly ended up with a baby human. Those are words from our "Abba" Father, the Daddy God who loves His children unconditionally, that He would even make a way through His Only Son Jesus, to die on a Cross so that we might live forever with Him.

Isaiah 44:2-5 - Thus says the Lord who made you from the womb, who will help you, Do not fear, O Jacob my servant; and you Jeshurun whom I have chosen. For I will pour out water on the thirsty land and streams on the dry ground; I will pour out My Spirit on your offspring and My blessing on your descendants; and they will spring up among the grass like poplars by streams of water. This one will say, I am the Lord's; and that one will call on the name of Jacob; and another will write on his hand, belonging to the Lord, and will name Israel's name with honor.

DECLARE THIS TRUTH OVER YOUR LIFE: I AM NOT A MISTAKE! I AM A CHILD OF GOD, FEARFULLY AND WONDERFULLY MADE!

Chapter Two

I went to spend the weekend with my beloved Papaw in my younger days. His house was scary, it was big, it smelled funny, it was old, and it was cluttered, so I really wasn't looking forward to that 2 day visit. I had become very accustomed to organization and stepping outside of my comfort zone was not my idea of fun. He woke me up before the sun on that Saturday morning with his booming voice, "Julie Anne, where are your play clothes?" Supposedly, he had gone into my suitcase, and finding nothing but frilly socks, patent leather shoes, bows, and dresses, he had decided to take matters into his own hands. Before I knew it, I was bundled into the front seat of his old pickup truck, milk and sugar with a splash of coffee in hand, and we were lumbering down the long driveway toward town. Being the only ones in the store at such odd hours, we had full reign of the aisles that he carried me down. Back at the register, he purchased for me a pair of jeans, some tennis shoes, and a few t-shirts with his meager wages, clothes fit for a fishing trip, a round of bowling, and a lesson in golf in the pasture behind his house.

That very same year, my paternal grandfather died of a heart attack. I called him Bandad. Mom and Dad had dropped my sister and I off at a strange place, a house we had never before been to with people we had never before seen (at least at the time I remember knowing they were complete strangers). They did so in a hurry. When they came back to get us, hours and hours later, fear had taken over my entire being. Abandonment was running wild through my mind and I was terrified. We were not allowed to go to Bandad's funeral, so for me there was no real closure. One day he was there, the next day he was gone, just like that. My Bana, my dear obsessive compulsive neat-freak of a grandmother, would never be the same.

Bana began taking us to the cemetery on weekends we would spend with her. We would "talk" to our grandfather for hours. She was sad and depressed and stayed that way for the next 25 years until she too passed away. When the trips to the graveyard became a regular event, I stopped going to see Bana on a regular basis. I longed for that Saturday morning with my maternal grandfather, Papaw. I believe God had me visit him afraid that weekend so I could truly understand what real peace felt like, so that I would have that memory to sustain me through moments of doubt and confusion for the rest of my life. I stopped my trips to the country with my Papaw out of the overwhelming guilt I had for my Bana that would send me to her house in a seemingly desperate attempt to stop the madness. I was just a small child, broken and confused.

To dispel these lies of the enemy placed in me long before I knew better so that I could do better and think better, I have to turn to the Word of God to find real satisfaction.

Another lie from the enemy entered my spirit those formidable years:

LIE #2 – What I learned from my grandmother is that sadness is a place to dwell and being a victim is part of life.

TRUTH #2 - IT IS WRITTEN: *"There is an appointed time for everything. And there is a time for every event under heaven – a time to give birth and a time to die; a time to plant and a time to uproot what is planted. A time to kill and a time to heal; a time to tear down and a time to build up. A time to weep and a time to laugh; a time to mourn and a time to dance" Ecclesiastes 3:1-4.*

God is clear to us that there is a time and season for all things so that means everything in life has an expiration date, including sadness and mourning.

God understands our pain and He gives us time to grieve, but then He expects us to get up and move on in what He is calling us to do next for His Kingdom purpose just as He instructed Samuel:

1Samuel 16:1 - Now the Lord said to Samuel, how long will you grieve over Saul, since I have rejected him from being king over Israel? Fill your horn with oil and go; I will send you to Jesse the Bethlehemite, for I have selected a king for Myself among his sons.

Nothing catches God by surprise; nothing we do or don't do, nothing another person does or does not do, absolutely nothing catches God off-guard. His plans and purposes continue to stand whether we do our part or not and the cycle of life continues to move on. We have a

—

destiny purpose to fulfill that we must do in obedience to God, lay our mourning aside at the foot of the cross, even as a sacrifice to God, and then get up and go do what He calls us to do. Our life is not predicated on another human's life.

People were meant to compliment other people, adding unto them. One human was never meant to complete another. Only God was meant to complete us. That is why when we seek fulfillment outside of God, we are always going to be disappointed because a human is incapable of fulfilling us completely and everlastingly. Only God can. We are given help mates, not soul mates. The Holy Spirit of God is our only Soul mate.

satan will lie to you and make you believe that if you don't continue to grieve, no one will remember your lost loved one. That is a lie because God knows that person by heart and will always remember them as will you. satan will tell you that you should continue to live in grief as a tribute to your love for that person; if you really loved them you will honor their memory by staying in a perpetual state of mourning. That is a lie designed to steal your joy and destroy your family and possibly your life.

The Bible tells us in both Mark 5 and Luke 8 about the story of a demon possessed man that Jesus healed. The man called himself Legion, for there were many demons in the man. As I was studying this story and looking up word meanings for deeper understanding, curious as to what would have opened this man up to such horrific demonic possession and the resulting self-inflicted harm, here is what I found.

The Greek word used here for tomb is *"mnema"*, "the man wandered the tombs of the Gerasenes", or as it states in other translations, the man was "living among the tombs". Wow, look at this. <u>*Mnema is the word for memorial or memories.*</u> Could it possibly be that in a deeper context the Lord is trying to warn us that the man opened himself up to demonic possession and the resulting destruction BY living among his memories, living in the past, living in his unresolved grief? I know the demons tormented me and certainly tried to cause me to destroy myself for 32 years because I was trying to live among my memories.

We can't always control what happens to us but we can control how we respond to it. Our response to pain is critical. Choose to stop focusing on what you don't have and focus on what God has given you and what He has left you with. Be thankful in all things. That isn't saying you are glad the tragedy happened, but thank God for what He is doing through it and how He will use it to His glory and our good. Choose to quit complaining and praise God for all He has brought you through. Call out to Holy Spirit, the Comforter, to give you peace that surpasses all understanding.

1 Thessalonians 5:16-24 - Rejoice always; pray without ceasing; in everything give thanks for this is God's will for you in Christ Jesus. Do not quench the spirit; do not despise prophetic utterances. But examine everything carefully; hold fast to that which is good; abstain from every form of evil. Now may the God of peace Himself sanctify you entirely; and may your spirit and soul and body be preserved complete, without blame at the coming of our Lord Jesus Christ. Faithful is He who calls you, and He also will bring it to pass.

—

11

Strength, faith, endurance – Your pain has a purpose.

Romans 8:28 - and we know that God causes all things to work together for good to those who love God, to those who are called according to HIS purpose.

When you stay focused on your loss you aren't staying focused on God. It then becomes a case of you putting more thought and value on your dead loved one than on God, thus making them an idol, which is sin against God and sickness to you. In some people's cases this leads to becoming addicted to their self-pity, grief-ridden story, telling and retelling it, being identified by it, and always being the victim in order to gain sympathy from others whether they consciously or subconsciously do it. That is one reason that people in the ancient days hired mourners for outward display of grief showing how sad they were at the loss of a person. We must not let grief debilitate us and stop us from moving forward in the fullness of our purpose in life and in the fullness of our joy in life. That is not honoring to our loved one or to God.

God gave you precious memories of precious time you had with your loved one, be thankful for what you had and not dwell on what you do not have today. For those of us who know the Lord as our Savior and whose loved ones knew the Lord, we will have a wonderful reunion one day in Heaven to look forward to. If you or your deceased loved one didn't have that salvation security, then you learn from their death as they would want you to, just as God's Word shows us in the story of the rich man and poor Lazarus in Luke 16:19-31. Secure your own salvation. Now is the only precious time you have left to ensure your own eternal security, enjoy the rest of your life in a personal relationship with Jesus, and then share Christ's plan of salvation with all others you love.

James 4:14 - Yet you do not know what your life will be like tomorrow. You are just a vapor that appears for a little while and then vanishes away.

Enjoy each moment of life. Don't waste it in despair over what you do not have. Life is filled with momentary and light afflictions when compared to the eternal glory we have in relationship with Christ. Cherish all that God has given you for any length of time you are given and then move forward eagerly into the newness of what He will bring into your life next.

Romans 8:16-18 - The Spirit Himself testifies with our spirit that we are children of God, and if children, heirs also, heirs of God and fellow heirs with Christ, if indeed we suffer with Him so that we may also be glorified with Him. For I consider that the sufferings of this present time are not worthy to be compared with the glory that is to be revealed to us.

Our response to pain is critical. Choose to stop focusing on what you don't have and focus on what God has given you and what He has left you with. Be thankful in all things.

<u>Chapter Three</u>

Isaiah 42:14 - For a long time I have kept silent, I have been quiet and held myself back. But now, like a woman in childbirth, I cry out, I gasp and pant.

Life was good. We were always surrounded by friends. Saturdays were spent at the Country Club where I first learned how to swim when my dad just threw me in the water to see what I was made of. I can remember the smell of chlorine outside mixed with the wafting air of grilling hamburgers coming from the inside. There was peace under a beautiful blue sky; the sound of children laughing and splashing in the pool filled the summer air. All the moms would be lined up like dominoes in lounge chairs, catching up on gossip, reading magazines, and yelling from time to time, "No, Susie!! Stay out of the deep end!" All the while, we would be playing Marco-Polo, or we would try to see who could do the most flips under water without taking a breath or whose handstand was the prettiest. The babies were always peeing in the baby pool, the Lifeguards were the cool high school kids whose parents were a little older than mine, and days were filled with laughter and joy! It was Louisiana summer heat!

I would stand at the fence that separated the pool area from the golf course and wait patiently until I saw the golf cart that carried my Daddy coming up the small path. I would hold on, expectantly, for him to make his next stroke before calling out to him. One wave is all I looked for. Anything more was a bonus. If he actually walked over to me, my heart would beat right out of my chest.

—

Saturday nights were spent at friends' houses where the young kids had control over the upstairs while we watched the high school teenagers get ready for dates and parties. The smell of bourbon, margaritas, and cigar smoke would waft into the open windows and fill the air outside where the adults were. Songs from Air Supply, Phil Collins, and other 80's crooners played on the record player.

My early years were made up of awesome memories! There were Peach Parades, dance recitals; late evenings riding bikes through the neighborhood, kick the can, and climbing trees were the norm. Then it happened...

My world was thrown up into the air and came back down in pieces, a puzzle completely broken. The jagged edges were strewn from one end of my perspective to another as I stood there, 10 years old, in wonder and confusion amongst the chaos. As I looked around at the pieces of my life falling from the sky, no piece matched up to another. In a matter of days, my dad was off to federal prison for embezzlement, his picture that was taken as Vice-President of the local bank was on the front page of countless newspapers, we lost our beautiful home, and I watched, in the pre-dawn hours of morning, my dad sit in a car and cry before leaving us behind to put the puzzle back together, a puzzle that no longer fit. There were so many pieces that couldn't be shoved into another piece no matter how hard I attempted with all my might

No more days at the Country Club waiting for his golf cart. No more Saturday night extravaganzas. No more anything. Every weekend at home for the weeks to follow I spent lying on the trampoline outside, looking up at the sky, and questioning a Being by the name of God that I couldn't see and didn't fully understand. The other weekends for the next 18 months, Christmas that year included, were spent on the road to Texarkana and many nights were spent at the LaQuinta Inn. I refused to even go outside to the playground during recess that year in 5th grade because of the horrible things that would come out of the mouths of the friends I once adored, things they would overhear their parents saying across the dinner table. I withdrew to the not so still parts of my mind and I contemplated, I questioned, and I anxiously watched and waited for relief that would never come.

LIE #3 – Life is not what you think and people you trust will leave in an instant because they don't love you enough to do right. Abandonment and Rejection are your new friends and they will never leave you.

TRUTH #3 - IT IS WRITTEN: *"a man of too many friends comes to ruin, But there is a friend who sticks closer than a brother." Proverbs 18:24.*

Jesus is that friend who will never leave you, the One who will stay with you through thick and thin, through the joys and pains in life. He is the One who will strengthen and comfort you, fill you like none other ever can. If anyone ever leaves the relationship, it will be you, not Him.

In Deuteronomy 31:6, God tells us that He will never leave us nor forsake us. However, He doesn't give us that assurance about any other human being that comes into our life no matter if they are Christian or not, no matter if they have the best of intentions. The truth is that all humans are flawed and fallible, they are subject to change of mind, change of motivation, change of situations, illness and death. They sin, they mess up, they make poor choices and mistakes, they/we all fall short of the glory of God and of being perfect in mind, will, power and emotion, as only He is perfect. Humans are just that…HUMAN. Although we often may find ourselves in the painful fall-out of another person's sin, whether it's their intention to hurt us or not, the actual sin that they perpetrate is against God, not us. They are the one who will suffer the full consequences of that sin, even far greater than any pain we feel from it.

Don't think that God's chosen don't sin too. David had been anointed by God to be King of God's people Israel and David still lusted after another man's wife, Bathsheba. King David set his sights on her, used his position and influence to seduce her into an adulterous affair, while her husband was off fighting in battle on behalf of David's army. When Bathsheba became pregnant with David's child that's when he knew word would get out so he had her husband, Uriah, sent to the front lines of the thickest battle in order to ensure he would be killed. That way David thought his sin would not be exposed – BUT GOD! The Lord knew all about it and exposed the darkness in David's heart in order to convict him unto repentance. What's done in secret will always come to light. God will expose it so we have to face and deal with it.

Always remember repentance is your means to forgiveness, healing and cleansing. God convicts unto repentance, the devil condemns you unto shame. David cried out for forgiveness, from his humble, broken, repentant heart, understanding that although Bathsheba and her husband Uriah were both harmed in the fallout of his sin, David's actual sin was disobedience to His holy and righteous God.

Psalm 51:4 - Against You, You only I have sinned and done what is evil in Your sight, so that You are justified when You speak and blameless when You judge.

Bottom line, no matter whether you feel victimized by another person's sin, the sin was against God, not you. There is power and victory in understanding that. Since it is between them and God, it lets you off the hook not to have to carry the weight of another person's sin; it gives you the freedom to see them for what they are, a human, albeit broken and/or sin-sick, and you forgive any wrong done to you and move forward in your life leaving the weight of their sin behind. Look, I can't even carry the weight of my own messes and sin. I sure am thankful the Lord has taught me not to try to carry the burden of others sins any longer, even if the wrong was done against me or hurt me in the fall-out.

When a person leaves a relationship, there can be many reasons for their departure from our lives, and it's not always a bad thing even if we love them and enjoy their company. Sometimes separations must come because the relationship itself may be holding one or both parties back from God's plan for your lives. Our perceived rejection by them may actually be God's protection or

—

simply Him having to push them or us out of the comfort nest in order for both parties to fulfill their destiny. We tend to want to hang on and get comfortable to make permanent fixtures out of relationships that God has deemed seasonal at best, even when we oftentimes know deep down that it is time to move forward. When a person moves on, most often than not, it isn't actually about them purposefully trying to harm us, and it may not be about us at all. It may just be about where they are in their own heart and life, whether they are doing the right thing or not.

Whatever the reason for the parting, bitterness is never the answer. It only makes you hurt more and prolongs your agony. God never tells us to un-love anyone. However, there are some people we will have to love from a distance as we move forward in our life & as God is bringing others into our lives to build new relationships with. Our pain comes when we try to un-love the folks who have hurt us or when their season in our destiny purpose has simply come to an end.

Surrender the pain, take time to heal and to self-evaluate to get stronger, better, wiser, and trust God to fill the open position in His time, His way, and with His person. Love God, love others, & He will heal your hurting heart as He adds others unto you, others who are now to become a part of your journey and who He will use to fulfill the roles of those left behind. Listen, my husband and I are prime examples of that and the Matthew 6:33 promise.

Here are some scriptures to help when you feel rejected or abandoned:

Hebrews 13:5
Deuteronomy 31:6
1 Samuel 12:22
John 14:18
Isaiah 4:10
John 14:1
Psalms 147:3
Galatians 6:7-10
Romans 8:35-39
Isaiah 54:10
2 Corinthians 1:3-4
Psalms 34:17
1 Peter 4:12-13
Isaiah 61:3

Love God, love others, & He will heal your hurting heart as He adds others unto you, others who are now to become a part of your journey and who He will use to fulfill the roles of those left behind.

Chapter Four

I lost my cat once. My mom ran over Callie while backing out of the driveway on the way to a bridal shower. We never made it to the bridal shower (maybe we did and I just can't remember). I was so overcome with that tragic loss of my little pet. We called Daddy off the golf course that bright, sunny day, away from his beloved pastime. I stood there in the doorway of our big home, in my frilly dress with my patent leather shoes and lace socks, with crocodile tears streaming down my face and staining the front of my smock as he packed up my friend in a small box and put her in the back of his truck to head back to the game he left behind that consumed him most weekends. I immediately objected, "But Daddy, what about the cow birds?" He quickly moved the box into a shed and he was off in a rush.

Late that afternoon as we stood under the clear sky, the sun barely peeking over the horizon, we buried my little friend. The three of us, Daddy, Jessie, and myself, were huddled in the back corner of our property near the fence. Jess and I fought back tears and prayed, "Now I lay me down to sleep, I pray the Lord my soul to keep, if I should die before I wake, I pray the Lord my soul to take." Daddy rolled his eyes and headed back inside to where dinner was waiting. As I watched his back as he walked away, I realized he was only doing his fatherly duty since mom had to deal with our sadness all day.

Fast forward some 8+ years. As you pass through time quickly with me, imagine a life torn; confusion, anger, and frustration all attaching themselves to us as we move through time and space. Fear, rejection, and abandonment join in. Doubt, worry, and self-loathing catch a ride on this crazy train. One quick turn around a bend creates one mess after another, and BOOM...we come to a complete halt and wreck on this journey. Beware of the whiplash as our train derails.

It's now August 25th, 1992, the third day of my sophomore year of high school. Dad has come from prison only a few years before and has become a ghost of a person. He isn't even the same and unfortunately never will be. We have moved from our small town and its big gossip to another town close by where a sense of freedom exists for all of us. I'm standing outside of a new school in the pouring down rain, standing before my mom who is completely broken, the light extinguished from her once shining green eyes. The questions immediately start inside my head as I ponder the look upon her sad face. I seem to tower over her, being 8 inches taller than her small frame anyway, but today she looks much smaller. She looks upon me and hesitates for a moment before speaking the words that will send a shockwave through our entire family, "There has been an accident." My reply, "It's Daddy." She nods her head in agreement, her tears mixed with the raindrops. I boldly say, "It wasn't an accident, was it? He did it himself." She barely nods her head as it hangs limply from her body. My dad has just committed suicide. Now I lay me down to sleep...

LIE #4 – **Nothing you do can keep those you love in your life; the best grades in school, the willingness to move to a new town without complaint, good behavior, none of it matters anymore. You are alone, left again to your own devices.**

TRUTH #4 - **IT IS WRITTEN:** *"The LORD also will be a stronghold for the oppressed. A stronghold in times of trouble; and those who know Your name will put their trust in You. For You O LORD, have not forsaken those who seek You." Psalm 9:9-10*

Many times, especially when occurring during childhood, people will internalize traumatic events, whether the trauma came from words, deeds or situations, believing the lie implanted by the enemy through the event that it is all their fault. They begin to think if they had only been different, better in some way, smarter, prettier, more lovable, more helpful, quieter, etc., then the event or the after-effects of it would have turned out differently and better too. This is how many people end up obsessive/compulsive about perfectionism.

Here's an example from a woman I met whose father and mother divorced when she was a very young child. Not understanding, as any child doesn't, the true scope of her parent's personal lives or the internal workings of their relationship, she bought into the lie of the enemy that somehow in their divorce she was at fault. The enemy set up the scene for her very well. She loved her Daddy and craved his affection and attention. Her father, a young man at the time, perhaps struggling with his own identity, and as she described the fruit of his Spirit to me, seemed to lack a relationship with the Lord. He was, by all accounts, preoccupied with his situation in life, his job, his unhappy marriage, and for whatever reasons the child did not know, she noticed that he stayed away from home more from where his wife and daughter were. Then once the parents had made the decision to live separately and divorce, the father packs up, family life as she knows it is all suddenly over and he leaves the home, leaving the 5 year old child behind with her mother. Immediately, abandonment and rejection and loneliness set up a new home in the child's heart and mind. The child only sees Daddy on scheduled weekend swap visits in HIS home now and then she is sent back at the appropriated time to her mom in THEIR home. This goes on, mom has issues of her own that the child has to live in until the opportune time comes for enemy take out, when the little girl is 13 years old, an impressionable age for sure. That enemy is a sly one – you have to watch him.

So here she is, barely a teen, Dad is driving her to school one day and she is happy to be getting this father/daughter time together. He looks over at her in what he perceives as a helpful way, but to her has been a mile marker event that cut and scarred her deeply, setting the wheels of destruction in full motion. Her Dad, being physically fit himself, and having another child with a physical condition that caused excess weight gain, believes he is simply suggesting to her that she may want to increase her exercise more and watch the amount of food she is eating because she seems to be putting on a few pounds. BAM! The enemy began to use every painful feeling of rejection, abandonment, loneliness, fear, self-worth lies to yell to her how she wasn't in the past but could be now Daddy's perfect little girl that he would love but only by starving, exercising, throwing up, taking diet drugs, laxatives, and diuretics right on into her adulthood. From that day on the woman battled with eating disorder and her obsession with perfectionism. She not only demanded it in herself but also began holding others to her unreal expectations to the point of absolute misery and destruction, leading her to other addictions too as she tried to numb out the pain. The shame, guilt, feelings of rejection and abandonment, as well as self-loathing continued. The harder we try to be perfect or to fabricate love where there is no love, and try to live up to the unrealistic expectations of perfectionism in ourselves or seek it in other humans, the worse the feelings of disgust and failure become.

Approval addiction is just as destructive and deadly as chemical addiction, it leads to a progressive agonizing death of the person that God created you to be. Many times people trade one addiction for another in their quest for freedom from a certain dependency they perceive as their problem. Many with approval addiction will begin to use other things, drugs, alcohol, shopping, sex, and food to try to feel better about their insecurities. The problem is not the specific addiction. The addiction is what they are trying to use as the solution to their problem. The real root problem is always a heart issue, not a behavior. The behavior is a result of the heart issue. Once you identify, remove and replace the heart issue with the Truth of God's Word by the power of the Holy Spirit in you, then the behavior will not be an issue for you any longer. That's what deliverance is. Jesus Christ is the Only Way, Truth,

& Life. He is the One who can give you a heart transplant to deliver you and heal you of all unrighteousness and emotional damage.

On the opposite side from Perfectionist is the "Can't Do Anything Right So Why Try" person. The enemy will use the same tactics to plant a lie but they feel helpless and hopeless to the point of just giving up on themselves, others, life. They give up on even trying – "What's the use, I can never be good enough, smart enough, beautiful enough, rich enough, popular enough so why even try?" Fears set in and some people, many beginning at the earliest ages in childhood, won't even try to do the simplest of things for fear of failure. They are so afraid of being embarrassed or shamed or being exposed as the failure they feel inside themselves, that they won't try to do or learn anything new. They get stuck in that fear and it becomes more controlling and confining until many never find success in any area of their life, especially jobs or relationships because of it. That just confirms the lie to them even more that they are a failure and will never amount to anything. They begin to believe that no one will ever like or love them, so it's better not to even try because if they try and fail they will be laughed at or rejected even more. They go through life shrinking back, hiding, peeping out from behind their wall of disappointment and fear with envy at others who have the courage to step out in faith, try something different, take the risk, grow and change their lives for the better. They truly believe that the blessings in life are for others but not for them so they stay stuck in their condition, their self-imposed bondage watching their life go by. Folks, if you want different in your life, you have to do different. Trust God and step out from behind the wall your hiding behind. Engage in life.

Proverbs 23:7 - For as he thinks within himself, so he is.

Scripture to counter the feelings of rejection by loved ones:

Psalms 94:14
Psalm 27:10
Matthew 28:20
Isaiah 62:4
2 Corinthians 4:9
1 Peter 5:7
Psalms 37:25
Deuteronomy 4:31
Isaiah 41:17
Psalms 91:14-15
Isaiah 49:15-16
Psalms 43:5
Deuteronomy 31:6

If you want different in your life, you have to do different.

<u>Chapter Five</u>

The day of my father's passing and the days to follow set me into motion in a direction I never intended to go. I stood at a crossroads and this tragedy carried with it massive potential to catapult me quickly to a new location in my heart and my mind. And it did. As I stood there, a road directly ahead, one to my right, one to my left, and the one behind from which I just came, I pondered. I heard loudly the voice behind me.

Isaiah 30:21 - Whether you turn to the right or to the left, your ears will hear a voice behind you, saying, "This is the way; walk in it."

It beckoned me ahead. I stood in a field, dirt roads at the cross, and heard the voice as plain as day, "This is the way. Please, come this way. I beg you not to allow this pain to consume you. Please listen to Me. Please just walk. All I am asking for is for you to take one step toward Me. I'm begging you, Julie." For a moment, I just sat down at the crossroad, shell shocked and confused.

As I sat, I watched the people pass in front of me, a line of simple folks who for a time disappeared and now here they were again, filing in solemn procession past the casket of a man who had long ago been forgotten.

satan crept into my heart, horrible anger filled my soul, and all I saw was injustice. The spiritual battle surrounding me ensued and evil won, but only for a time. Twenty-two years to be exact. I stood up at the crossroad and for those twenty-two years I walked back and forth, wandering from the right to the left, always passing the crossroad and briefly stopping to look back to the past then peering into the other direction which was quite unfamiliar toward a future that I couldn't' even imagine or fathom. So, I just kept wandering.

I picked up hitchhikers along the way, lonely other souls that pulled me in the direction they wanted me to go. I stopped at rest stops on my journey, only to head back out with more baggage than I could carry. I ate at roadside diners, eating more than my fill of the wrong kind of food. Yet, I always stopped to ponder the crossroad.

The day my dad left, I stood on one side of the door and watched him pace and cry and wander in his own mind. I didn't go to him, instead I cried from the other side of the window in the door and I then walked away. The next time my curiosity peaked and I looked outside; he was gone, never to be seen again. The cross road came into view; I took a wrong turn, and began my journey down a beat up road full of potholes and detours.

LIE #5 – It's your entire fault. You should have gone to him in his most desperate time of need. You are just like him. Your life will be so full of questions that you will go to unstoppable lengths to find answers, and you, too, will die a lonely, early death.

TRUTH # 5 - IT IS WRITTEN: *"Your eyes have seen my unformed substance; And in Your book were all written the days that were ordained for me, when as yet there was not one of them. How*

precious also are your thoughts to me, O God!
How vast is the sum of them! If I should count
them, they would outnumber the sand. When I
awake, I am still with You." Psalms 139:16-18

As you see in Psalms 139:16 God Himself ordains the number of days we live and even goes so far as to write them in His book before He ever even creates us. His purpose for us is clearly to prosper us, to live an abundant life with Christ as the center of our lives, to glorify Him, to spend time in relationship with Him and to make Him be in the forefront of our heart, mind, family, job, hobbies, friendships, everything while we are here on this earth. Sadly many of us choose otherwise.

It is amazingly mind blowing to me that God thinks about each one of us more times than there are grains of sand, and that's assuming the Psalmist just meant sand on the Earth itself. NASA may tell us there is sand on other planets as well. Do you actually understand how many grains, not beaches full of grains of sand, but the actual grains of sand themselves there are on the Earth? It's even more times than that that God thinks about you and me. I love the old hymn that says about Jesus, "When You were on the cross, I was on Your mind". That kinda puts that in a new perspective doesn't it? How can you possibly think you are destined to live and die a lonely, miserable, and then early death. When is an early death anyways?

2 Peter 3:8 - But do not forget this one thing, dear friends, with
the Lord a day is like a thousand years, and a thousand years are
like a day.

———

Psalm 90:4 - A thousand years in your sight are like a day that has just gone by, or like a watch in the night.

2 Peter 3:9 - The Lord is not slow in keeping his promise, as some understand slowness. Instead he is patient with you, not wanting anyone to perish, but everyone to come to repentance.

God has given us all the warning in His Word and through His Prophets, Preachers and Teachers. He tells us to be on the watch, be prepared, to make ready for His second coming or our going to Him, whichever God has ordained to happen first. We are the ones who do not heed that warning. We are the ones who live our lives as if this is all there is. We are the ones who want to disregard Him and downright ignore Him but yet complain when we believe He is somehow short-changing us on our number of days and the quality thereof.

Who determines what early death really is? Is there an age appropriate to death? Seems to me that many of the most miserable people I've seen are the very ones who complain the most as they either get older, live longer or if they think they are coming closer to the end. Suddenly they want to stay here the longest yet resent it the most when others go before them. Why is that? My son was 22, my sister 58, and my Dad 74 when each died in the physical. Each upon death by the blood of the Lamb Jesus and by the words of their testimonies and by the love test as it tells us in 1 John, bore fruit that they were born again into new life, Spiritual life, to live for eternity in Heaven with God. That was God's goal for them. That was my ultimate hope for each of them as someone who loved them. They just got there sooner than I had expected. But even in my pain, I was happy for them, knowing they were

34

in that perfect place of life everlasting in the very Presence of their Lord. Regardless of the time or circumstances of how they each arrived at their eternal destination, I'm convinced they made it, because they were convinced they were going to make it, so who am I to say what an early death is. As far as I see in the Bible, my loved ones there are more alive than I am this side of Heaven so we are just in two different locations right now until the great reunion day one day when I arrive. There are many, myself included, who know that a prolonged period of time on this evil earth is not all it's made out to be if you truly know Christ as your Savior. Now if you don't then I understand your wanting time to get things right and that's the only explanation I have for those who fear death, the unknown afterlife, because they are unsure of where they will spend their eternity. None of us have the promise of our next breath so get it right with Jesus right now before you read the next sentence of this book – PLEASE!

We, and others, often unknowingly speak death and curses over our lives and the lives of others, generational curses are set in motion, but our God is greater. We can recognize, repent, renounce, and reactivate the blessings over our own lives and the lives of our family for generations to come.

Revelations 12:14-17 - The woman was given the two wings of a great eagle, so that she might fly to the place prepared for her in the wilderness, where she would be taken care of for a time, times and half a time, out of the serpent's reach. Then from his mouth the serpent spewed water like a river, to overtake the woman and sweep her away with the torrent. But the earth helped the woman by opening its mouth and swallowing the river that the dragon had spewed out of his mouth. Then the dragon was enraged at the woman and went off to wage war against the rest of her offspring — those who keep God's commands and hold fast their testimony about Jesus.

As we continue in our stinking thinking we begin sending poisonous words spewing into the atmosphere, words that curse our lives and the lives of others such as our own children and their children's children for generations to come.

Psalm 21:10 - You will destroy their descendants from the earth, their posterity from mankind.

Whole families have been strategically wiped out by the enemy. He will send the spirit of negativity, spirit of heaviness, spirit of depression, and spirit of suicide to systematically destroy one generation to the next to wipe out the seed and discontinue the lineage. Negative thoughts and negative words are very dangerous. If he can steal a person's joy, he has stolen their strength.

Nehemiah 8:10 - Go and enjoy choice food and sweet drinks, and send some to those who have nothing prepared. This day is holy to our Lord. Do not grieve, for the joy of the Lord is your strength.

The key to overcoming negativity, heaviness, depression and even suicidal thoughts is to take your thoughts captive with the power of praise and gratitude. If you think on things they begin to magnify and become overwhelming. All actions begin with a thought so you must not even entertain negative thoughts or you will be consumed with fear and doubt, two of the enemy's biggest tools.

Isaiah 61:1-4 says - The Spirit of the Lord God is upon ME, because the Lord has anointed ME to bring good news to the afflicted; He has sent ME to bind up the brokenhearted, to proclaim liberty to captives and freedom to prisoners; to proclaim the favorable year of the Lord and the day of vengeance of our God; to comfort all who mourn, to grant to those who mourn in Zion, giving THEM a garland instead of ashes, the oil of gladness instead of mourning, the mantle of praise instead of a spirit of fainting. So THEY will be called oaks of righteousness, the planting of the Lord, that HE may be glorified. Then THEY will rebuild the ancient ruins, THEY will raise up the former devastations; and THEY will repair the ruined cities, the desolations of many generations.

Break the generational curses in your family by Praise – put on your mantle of Praise and share it for others to hear the good news of freedom! Praise God out loud, speak Truth found in God's Word, quote scripture, sing praises and worship Him. Do not isolate. Get out around others, fellowship with like-minded believers. Listen, you can always find some kind of worship or fellowship going on somewhere. Why do we think we are only allowed to attend one church? We as believers are the church. Go wherever you find others. The Lord says where two or more are gathered together in His Name, there He is also. Don't allow yourself to speak death and destruction, curses of negativity, out of your mouth. If it isn't edifying God, don't say it and certainly don't think and dwell on it. Refocus on positive life giving, life building things.

Romans 8:6 - The mind set on the flesh is death, but the mind set on the spirit is life and peace.

Proverbs 18:21 - Death and life are in the power of the tongue, and those who love it will eat its fruit.

John 10:10 - the thief comes to steal, kill and destroy; I have come that they may have life, and have it to the full.

<u>Chapter Six</u>

Vulnerability – capable of being physically wounded; open to attack or damage.

After the funeral, we moved back to Ruston, Louisiana. We moved back into our home that we hadn't even had the chance to completely pack up from the quick move that Dad had us undergo. I walked back into the high school I dreaded, surrounded by the friends I didn't trust. I made it through my sophomore year and plunged into school work to get by. On the outside, I was holding it together. I was on the dance line, I had a ton of fair weathered friends, I was a straight "A" student, I was published in "Who's Who Among American High School Students", a National Honor Society member. Friday night football games and Saturday afternoon tailgate parties on Louisiana Tech campus, surrounded by lights and people, were the highlights of my weekends. The summer evenings before my junior year of high school were spent wherever in the woods we could find in the woods to have bonfires without getting caught. That's where it happened…

On the inside I was a jumbled mess. I was seeking solace from relationships. I was addicted to my story first, the approval of others second. It's why I made the horrible decision to have sex for the first time with a boy, a popular upcoming senior, in the backseat of my car in the middle of the woods on that hot June evening. I did it to get approval, to feel loved, to be accepted. I did it to get a fix, to heal my broken heart, to know that I was liked by this very handsome fellow. I did it to fill a void that had been left empty less than a year before.

Four months later, I walked into a Subway on a Friday afternoon after classes to get a snack before the big game. The smell that wafted from the restaurant that used to make me hungry at this point caused me to instantaneously lose my lunch all over the floor. I wasn't in tune with my body and was suffering from a horrible eating disorder that left me emaciated on a good day so I had no idea what to make of my current situation. The very next Friday, upon leaving the pep rally and dancing my heart out before our entire student body, still dressed in my Bearcat Belle uniform, my best friend and I went back to the very same spot in the woods with a pregnancy test in hand. Bloomers around my ankles, ants biting my feet, I peed on a stick and I grew up…right then and there.

How was I going to tell my mother? She had been dating a wonderful man for a few months, a police officer from another parish. I stayed on her like white on rice about not having sex before marriage. I used to guilt her with the fact that we (my sister and I) needed for her to set a good example for us to follow. And here I was, now sitting alone after the football game in my peach and green room, looking out the window with tears streaming down my face, pondering how I was going to break her heart. Hadn't we suffered enough already? The gravity of the situation was more than I could bear.

I finally mustered the courage to go tell her the impending news. We cried together, sitting on the bed she once shared with my dad. After a long discussion, hours upon hours of her begging me and attempting with all her might to talk me out of what MY plan was, we moved forward with the only thing I knew to do. It was my only option. The following week, she checked me out of school and we headed to the big city. That hour long drive seemed to take days.

We arrived at our destination, only to be met by picketers, people spitting in my direction, signs held up for all to see. They were not silent. Insults, ridicule, slander were all being hurled in my direction and hitting my heart with so much force that I thought I would die right there on the sidewalk. I stepped foot into the darkness, windowless, and void. No light of day shined into the recesses of my heart or into the coldness of the room in which I stepped into. Sadness enveloped the whole space like a cold, wet blanket and the eyes of each individual that mine met were empty…lost…hurt.

After tests were run and a sonogram done by a heartless nurse, my mom and I were ushered through the silence into a room with a table. We took our seats across the huge table from a counselor. She showed me a picture of my unborn child and the begging ensued once again. "Please don't do this, Julie. You are halfway there. We will help you. PLEASE, Julie." I wasn't hearing any of it. I played on my mom's guilt over losing dad and won. I was already past the point of no return. I had already placed huge pieces of fleshy sinew over my broken heart and I was done.

The procedure (if you want to even call it such a nice name) took two solid days. The night in the hotel room after they had to dilate my cervix was excruciating, physically and mentally. The spiritual side of me was

—

41

from that point on forever locked in a corner deep inside of me, placed there by me, locks put on so tight there was no room for conviction or escape. I then retreated to the darkness in order to get past what was taking place in my body. I went on a trip, and part of me never returned. That second day is so vivid in my mind. I was being shuffled from one dark room to another with no noise but the sound of my beating heart and the cries and screams coming from the rooms that I couldn't see. We were lined up like ducks in a row on gurneys, not sure what was around the corner, but knowing that it was going to hurt every single part of us. I remember the pain I felt in my heart, the longing I had for a touch or a word from a kind person, the way my senses changed when the I.V. was placed in my hand, the void that I saw in the eyes of the women that would have the courage to meet my gaze. I remember the searing pain and the screaming that I didn't even recognize that came from the inside of me. Then more shuffling, from one dark room to another. If only the walls could talk.

I was back on the football field, donning my sparkly outfit and doing jump splits in front of the newly named Homecoming Court debutants within two weeks. I didn't know who knew what and I didn't care. The summer before my junior year of high school set in motion a chain of events that would completely reshape the outlook on my life. I found out that October that there was a list, a horrific list, of the most vulnerable girls in high school put out by a fraternity at our school. They had the summer of '93 to bed down a girl on that list for bragging rights and a prize. My name was at the top of that list because my father had just died.

LIE #6 – You are a whore, and no one wants to be your friend. You will never find true love because of the horrible things you have done. You might as well continue with this journey because it's the only way you will ever find satisfaction from anyone. You will never escape this pain. You are not worthy of anyone looking to you for love. You are a murderer.

TRUTH #6 - IT IS WRITTEN: *"He saved us, not on the basis of deeds which we have done in righteousness, but according to His mercy, by the washing of regeneration and renewing by the Holy Spirit whom He poured out upon us richly through Jesus Christ our Savior." Titus 3:5-6*

Thank God for Truth or none of us could ever be forgiven and saved! It plainly says it is not on the basis of deeds which we have done, it's all on the basis of what Jesus has done in our place, for us to be able to be saved. Hallejulah!

Holy Spirit convicts us of all our unrighteousness – unto repentance – so that we become aware of our sin, repent of it which is to recognize it as sin, ask Jesus to forgive us for it, turn from it, that is to stop doing it, and go forward in a new position, a new direction away from that sinful thing. That's how we grow into the character of Christ, more like Him, by being confronted with our sin so we can change.

The total opposite which is a perversion of conviction that many Christians don't even seem to understand or recognize is that condemnation is not of Christ. It is <u>the devil</u> who <u>condemns unto shame</u>.

I heard a very wise Pastor say once that shame is not just a feeling; it is a condition that can become an illness. Upon hearing that the Lord reminded me how very evident that is through the lives of so many broken people I see every single day. He also reminded me that an illness left untreated can very quickly lead to death. That shame the enemy is constantly pouring into our thoughts will cause us to do unthinkable things in order to cover it and hide from it. But shame dies when Truth is told from the safety of the Cross. When we give our shame over to God, first to be made right with Him and then to be used to glorify Him and help others, He will destroy the shame and replace it with joy and peace.

I love this saying and I used it in my own life so often as I was learning how to forgive myself for my own past. A friend told me "when satan tries to remind you of your past, you just remind him of his future". Bottom line is, don't even entertain those thoughts. We are victorious in Christ! Grace is greater than all my sin and yours.

Romans 8:1-4 - Therefore there is no condemnation for those who are in Christ Jesus. For the law of the Spirit of life in Christ Jesus has set you free from the law of sin and of death. For what the Law could not do, weak as it was through the flesh, God did: sending His own Son in the likeness of sinful flesh and as an offering for sin, He condemned sin in the flesh so that the requirement of the Law might be fulfilled in us, who do not walk according to the flesh but according to the Spirit.

———

There is no condemnation in Christ Jesus. He frees us from all our unrighteousness. A life's story, no matter how heinous, that is given to Christ to be used to God's glory, giving Him the total access to it, to use however and wherever He chooses, trusting Him by faith that He is in total control of it, as He paid the price for it, it's His now, that story my friends will not ever have any more shame and condemnation attached to it. You can bank on that.

Almighty God, the Creator of Heaven and Earth and all that dwells therein knew every single sinful thought, word and deed that you and I and everyone else would ever do in our entire lifetime even unto eternity. He figured it all in to the Cross. He figured it in to your destiny and to the destiny of His Kingdom. That is a powerful realization. You, nor I, nor even the devil have the power to mess up God's plan and purpose, no matter how jacked up we all are. He figured your story in to how He would use it at just the right time to His glory, your good and the good of others who hear and find their own hope in Christ through it. Give it to Him and see.

The world will try to label us and call us so many ugly names all in an attempt to tear down, to heap shame and ridicule us, to destroy our self-value, to steal our joy, our hope, and our faith in God's ability to forgive us and use us. It all comes from the enemy who is the accuser. Yes he brings on the shame that we allow to quickly go from a thought to a feeling, from a feeling to a condition of our heart, then we act out of that shame to become the circumstance of our life, an illness of our mind, will and emotions, rendering us useless, a victim, locked away from our destiny, trapped in our fears of what others must think of us.

We, as Julie demonstrates above in the Lie she believed, will believe those ugly names and begin to identify with them and call ourselves those names and even far worse. But God! When He washes you white as snow, He will give you a new name, one fitting of His most prized possession.

When He cast our sin as far as the east is from the west and chooses to remember it no more, when we have been grafted into His family, with His Name and under His righteousness, the world can call us whatever they so mistakenly throw our way, but we do not ever have to receive that mistaken identity ever again. We have been adopted into the family of God where no human or demonic judge can ever reverse that decision. Our new name is found written in the Lamb's Book of Life, our heart is changed forever and our character is being rebuilt in the likeness of Christ.

Post Abortion Grief

After counseling many women who have had abortions, and after living through the horrifying after-effects myself, I began to see a clear pattern of behaviors in all of us to varying degrees. These behaviors also greatly resembled the patterns of behaviors that I began to see in those following molestation and rape. I began to research to see what other information or common characteristics I could find because quite frankly for many years I just thought it was me and I was crazy without cause. But to the contrary, it was more unresolved grief with deep lingering effects.

Here is a brief summary of what I found and personally know to be true. Many Psychologists and Doctors recognize Post-Abortion Syndrome (PAS) as a form of Post-Traumatic Stress Disorder (PTSD). Regardless of whether the women believed they were doing the right thing in having the abortion at the time of the event or felt forced into it by circumstances or another person, many women suffer the same after-effects in some degree and fashion. PTSD often occurs after an individual has suffered an event so stressful and so traumatic that this person is unable to cope with this experience in a normal manner. Many times they are unable to resume their lives where they had left off prior to the event. It becomes a mile marker in their life. Instead, they experience a variety of reactions that do not go away merely with the passage of time. The symptoms vary from case to case, and sometimes these reactions may not arise until years after the event. Seemingly unrelated things can even trigger the reactions and depending on added stress levels, some reactions can intensify.

Some common symptoms found in women suffering Post-Abortion syndrome are: depression and thoughts of suicide; sad mood; sudden and uncontrollable crying; deterioration of self-esteem; disruption in interpersonal relationships; sleep, appetite, and sexual disturbances; promiscuous sexual behavior and/or fear of or refusal to have sexual relations or feelings of disgust regarding sex; reduced motivation; anniversary syndrome; an increase of symptoms around the time of the anniversary of the abortion and/or the due date of the aborted child; re-experiencing the abortion; preoccupation with becoming pregnant again; anxiety over fertility and childbearing issues; disruption of the bonding process with present or future children; survival guilt; the sorrowful resignation that "it's me or you, and I chose me"; development of eating disorders; alcohol and drug abuse.

I urge anyone who has suffered from one of the greatest lies of destruction that the enemy has used in our age – abortion, to know dear sister that you can be free from the sin of your past – yes, even abortion. There are websites with additional help and information.

Chapter Seven

Mentally abusive relationships in my life were born out of a depth of insecurity that is almost unimaginable; a feeling of such hopelessness for a future with anyone. I had a desire to run as far away as possible and I was intent on finding someone who would take me to the far reaches of the earth.

It was my senior year of college and I was on a roll. I was working full time and had a full school load taking as many courses as they would allow. I was also stuck in a relationship that nearly cost me everything. I was slowly adding one link after another to an already heavy chain that hung from my neck and was attached directly to the enemy.

I would drive from my boyfriend's house every day back to my home town, but I wasn't allowed to take any detours, not even to see my parents. Until...

It was a February afternoon, I was home alone in a house I shared with him for a few days and my heart exploded to see my family. I called mama to tell her I was coming to see them for the first time in nearly 6 months. It didn't go unnoticed that for months I would come to my hometown to attend classes at the University and not even stop to see my parents because I was on such a tight schedule which was produced for me out of my boyfriend's own insecurities. My mom had since remarried to a wonderful man who took every step to make sure we were provided for. He became my dad almost instantly and I was so grateful that she was no

---

longer alone. It became my reason for justifying not stopping in to even say hello, much less have dinner or lunch with my family.

That day in February, I was going to taste freedom from the dining room table surrounded by my loved ones who missed me so. Freedom from lack of trust, from insecurity, from loneliness, from being told what to do, how to do it, in what time frame to do it in, from how to act, what to wear, where to go. I would have an opportunity to rest in the arms of my mom and eat from the table of family unity. I was one month away from graduation and my very life and all I dreamed of was slowly slipping through my fingers because of my obsession with one human being. I was seeking solace, comfort, and security from this man and it never came.

No one but my mother knew I was coming home. Just as I was pulling into town, she was leaving to go in the direction from which I just came. She was headed that way to pick my awesome new dad up from the airport after a police officer convention and I was headed her direction for healing and restoration. I made it home to an empty house and went straight to dinner and drinks with a few friends at an establishment I normally didn't grace with my presence. I was completely out of my normal routine. I ordered my first drink of the night, put my quarters in the pool table, and got busy about my own business. Moments later, I looked up to see a man who was like a brother to me, a police officer on the force with my dad, darken the doorway. This man had been to our house on many occasions when mom would cook for the young, single officers on the late night shift. We were family. He stood there, tears streaming down his face, white as a ghost, dressed in full officer gear and fear completely took over my whole being as I looked upon him with wonder and interest, pool stick in hand, as he stared at me. I recognized that something wasn't right and I was paralyzed. Time stopped briefly as I tried to conjure up in my mind what in the world was going on. I instantly put on my mask to let everyone know I was ok and headed out the door in a brief stroll to keep from running full speed ahead.

"There has been an accident," were his first words once I was face to face with my friend.

"Is it dad? Papaw?" I inquired.

"It's your mom." These are the same words spoken to me when my first dad passed away. I was in vice grip in that moment and I believe I stopped breathing all together.

"We don't know if she survived. Please come with me, Julie." I heard those words but they didn't register as I walked around in circles trying to remember where I parked my car.

"What happened? Where was she? Are you telling me my mom is dead?"

"COME WITH ME, Julie."

Immediately, and by no act of my own, I was shuffled into a police car and whisked away, traveling toward the interstate at high speed through our quiet little town. Upon our arrival to the on ramp, I noticed another police car, blue lights blazing. I saw another friend and brother standing next to it in full uniform and we came to a screeching halt. I was pulled out of one car and put into another. One police officer was driving, another in the front seat, and one in the back seat with me and we were

51

off, over 100 miles an hour directly toward the scene of the accident all the while sirens going on above my head.

I first took notice of the line of red brake lights ahead. As we got closer and closer, my heart felt as if it would beat right out of my chest. I was in the backseat screaming out to a God I had long forgotten, "Why did you make me an orphan? WHY??? Why did you take my parents away?" What I saw next took my breath away. Any ounce of strength that still remained in my body left in an instant and I was a crumpled mess on the floor of the police car. A crumpled version of my mom's vehicle, illuminated by the lights of emergency vehicles and cars that were backed up for miles, sat on the wrong side of the interstate, on the side of the interstate that she wasn't traveling down. We drove past the line of cars through the median and stopped briefly for the officers to have a short exchange with the emergency workers. I begged them to let me out since I couldn't get out of the car myself. I was in the back of a police car after all. They let me out and I began to run through the median toward the crumpled mess on the other side only to be caught by a faceless person. I couldn't see past the pain at that point. I was put back into the car and we were off toward the hospital.

I wandered through that hospital, shell shocked and confused. I rounded a corner and ran into my dad. He took me to see my sweet mom who was hooked up to machines but still alive! The blipping of the machines began to give me a raging headache as I looked upon my limp mother whose own head was the size of a watermelon. Six months she would eventually call that hospital and rehabilitation center her home, but she was alive and breathing and for that I was grateful.

———

I was charged with spending the night with her in the hospital only days before my college graduation. I spent the night with a different version of my mom. She was awake but her head injuries had caused her to forget everything, including how she used to act. It definitely wasn't my mommy under the covers writhing in pain and cussing under every breath. I mentally checked out of that room and kept on with my obsession with this man and attempted to no avail to forget that I was even in that room.

One week later, I graduated from Louisiana Tech University with a Bachelor's degree. My mom wasn't there, that man wasn't there, and I walked across the stage with no purpose to speak of...alone. After graduation, I went to the hospital in my cap and gown and walked into a room with a woman who didn't recognize me. She didn't even know my name. I used it as another excuse and put another nail in my coffin that I was building for myself in the spiritual. I ran to the closest big city I could and landed a job that paid well. I found a place, bought a car, and settled in for what would be the most terrifying ride of my life.

LIE #7 – You are so selfish. You can't do anything right. Where are your feelings, your compassion? Who do you think you are to just run away from your family when they need you the most? You are not all that. You will fail. No one loves you. You can't even keep a man in your life. I hate you, so run away...it's your only

option. Don't ever stop running. It is your only way out of your miserable mind.

TRUTH #7 - IT IS WRITTEN: *"Draw me after you and let us run together! The king has brought me into his chambers. We will rejoice in you and be glad; we will extol your love more than wine. Rightly do they love you." Song of Solomon 1:4*

There are two things that really jumped out at me here in the lie.

One, we are all selfish apart from Christ. In our natural flawed human heart state we are selfish. God tells us that the heart is deceitful above all things. It is only through our relationship with Christ, Him in us, and through our own life sufferings that teach us compassion for others, that we come to feel empathy for others who are going through pain and suffering.

The second thing that I see so often today is a world full of runners, a lack of staying power, sticking it out through good times and bad. There doesn't seem to be a clear understanding or desire for commitment among most people in our world today. Our natural tendency when faced with hardship, pain, shame, and guilt is to run from it rather than running to God, into His arms for direction, peace and comfort. But to run away from our troubles does no good because we do not address and apply solutions to our problem, we only add to them by taking not only our original problem, but our shame and guilt with us to the next location, leaving behind broken pieces for others to either deal with or hurt from. Even if we don't think of the ones left behind, we are still not at peace in our new location because we are always fearful that we will be exposed for the awful person we believe we are, trying so hard for others not to find out about it. We can't enjoy the new place because in our mind and often our behaviors, we are still acting out of the old place.

Again, repentance is your healing balm. In order to rid yourself of shame, pain, and guilt; you must first rid yourself of the sin, repent and be made clean of the offense that brought on the shame. If your "friends" are accusing you, attacking you, reminding you of what you have done, or leaving you because of it, they really weren't true friends indeed. While true friends will be honest with us and hold us accountable by not covering for us and confronting us in love about our sin, it is not anyone's place to drag us through the mud and throw accusations against us. But you remember that two wrongs don't make a right. You be the bigger person and you forgive them for what they are doing and PRAY FOR THEM. Let the words of our Lord ring in your heart and mind "Father, forgive them, for they know not what they do." They will be held accountable for their own sin. When you repent of your part, you forgive and pray for them so that you from then on, "Let God be true and every man a liar".

After Job's "well -meaning" friends threw accusations and shame on him, they abandoned him to what they thought was his end. But Job forgave them & prayed for them as God told him to, and it was Job in the end that got the double portion of blessing by doing that.

Job 42:10 - *The Lord restored the fortunes of Job when he prayed for his friends, and the Lord increased all that Job had twofold.*

Hmmm, it never mentions again in the bible what happened to Job's long gone shame throwing friends.

And again, PRAISE, PRAISE, PRAISE God! Speak scripture over yourself of who you are to Christ and you will begin to believe you are who He says you are, and you will begin to see that it doesn't matter what the world thinks about you.

Chapter Eight

I partied. I was single, living alone in a big city with no restrictions, working a full time job, and I was broken beyond repair. I wore a mask everyday just to survive, putting an apparatus over my face and heart everyday like it was makeup and I had grown quite accustomed to it. I had run away from everything I had ever been taught and directly into the arms of the enemy. I walked right into his camp and pitched a tent. On the outside, I was a beautiful, confident, strong-willed woman of nobility. On the inside, I was a broken vessel, shattered by the circumstances of life, beaten by the lies in my heart, and hopeless. I built shelters in the strongholds of my heart and became very comfortable and complacent in slavery and oppression. Everything that came at me negative was welcomed because excuses became the nails that built my house of failure.

I was the top sales person at my finance job, the highest ranking sales person in 3 states, but I was a female working in a man's world. When the Big Boss would ride in on his horse (his fine Mercedes Benz) from Baton Rouge, I would be required to hold down the fort at work so that the men I worked with could go play golf with the MAN. My accolades and hard work didn't matter. I was still looked at as a slave to the desk when it was time to go have fun, because I was a girl and I didn't golf. In walks "Rejection" and "Injustice" and I became very bitter and angry. It made me want to go take my bras and go burn them in the streets as generations of liberated women had done before me. It became another excuse to "show them."

—

Going to church wasn't even close to making an appearance on my "to do" list. I was too busy getting caught up by the night life and the bright lights of the big city, making friends in the clubs who pushed strange looking pills towards me that took me into realms of ecstasy and a new spiritual awakening was on the horizon. I felt free, like I could conquer the world. On more than one occasion, I would walk out of the club to see the sun peeking over the horizon only to put something else up my nose just to be able to make it to work. Alcohol, bright lights, loud music, men, dancing, and drugs were my new normal and I finally felt like I had truly escaped the hell of my former life. I was alive in a new way. I had completely shut myself out of reality and so began a new mission to kill myself slowly and seek answers to question I would never find.

I met my first husband at a bar. I wish I could say I met him at work or at church but that isn't where I spent all my time. I had already spent myself enough at the expense of myself. I was immediately drawn to his peace. It was absolutely love at first sight. I had never before laid eyes on someone so handsome and beautiful. He radiated confidence and strength as he walked in from the rain and I looked up and caught his eye. I will never forget that night as long as I live as I sat there across from my bartender friend girl in an empty establishment donning overalls, a tank top, and no makeup. I was there studying for one of the hardest tests I would ever take. I had already been convicted in my heart that I wasn't living right and was seeking to get into the Air Force Officer Training School so I could have some solid guidance in my life and do something different for myself. I was also very much attracted to the fact that men would salute me. I got a huge kick out of that!

I remember passing notes to my friend, Rachel, inquiring about the handsome man with the rain-slicked buzz cut, the good looking fellow who just walked in. I felt like I was in junior high school in an instant and my plain face showed every emotion as I blushed in the dim lights.

First came the rejection. Seriously, why did I think I was even close to attractive sitting there so plainly dressed? Rachel spoke soft words to him about me as she handed him his first drink and his words were, "No, thanks." Then it became a conquest won and the days, weeks, and months to follow were a dream come true. The partying never stopped and secrets ran rampart in this new relationship. Almost immediately, the yoke of co-dependency was tightened upon my neck and I faltered under the weight of it. I moved in with this handsome man within weeks and shortly thereafter he left on a mission to help the United Nations in Morocco, Africa.

Those six months proved to be my downfall as I did everything I could to escape the loneliness. I was no longer a self-sufficient, independent business woman who dabbled in the clubs on the side. I was a train wreck, merely trying to survive, keeping secrets even from myself. Lying to everyone became the norm and I could barely keep up with the words spewing from my own mouth on a daily basis. Keeping up pretenses became a chore and I was exhausted.

Shortly after his return stateside, I found out I was pregnant...again. My atheist boyfriend said to me, "I'm trying to get on at this base in Kansas City. I want to fly that fancy plane. They are a religious bunch up there and it will ruin my career to have a pregnant girlfriend. I won't stand a chance." That was all I needed to hear.

We didn't speak to one another on the way to the very same clinic I had been to before. Nothing had changed about the place and I was almost comfortable in my quest walking into the darkness. We didn't even make eye contact as I stepped into the rooms that would once again consume my heart. We didn't acknowledge what was taking place and I went through the familiar motions and barely remember the pain or the details because I blocked it from my mind. I was getting pretty good at forgetting.

He ushered me upstairs upon arriving back at "his" house that I just happened to live in and left me there. After hours of sitting in excruciating pain, I finally crawled down the stairs in an attempt to find some water. I collapsed on the floor at the bottom of the stairs and interrupted the game he and his friend were watching. I spent the next 20 minutes, on the floor, listening to the accusations and condemnation spewing out of the mouth of our "so-called" friend who stood over me with a pointing finger. He had plenty to say as my boyfriend stood by, quiet as a church mouse.

I was unable to move, mainly from the pain in my heart. I asked for the phone, picked it up, and called my friend from a bar I frequented and she came to my rescue. She put me in the car and got me high before we even left the driveway. I was no longer using for fun, now it was a means to numb myself from the pain of who I was becoming.

LIE #8 – You piece of crap. Everybody hates you. You are so worthless. You have NO meaning to your life other than to bring pain to others. You ruin everything you touch. You are not worthy of a relationship with anyone. You are not worthy to be a mom. You are the most unlovable person on the planet.

TRUTH #8 - IT IS WRITTEN: *"Then she called the name of the Lord who spoke to her, 'You are a God who sees'; for she said, 'Have I even remained alive here after seeing Him." Genesis 16:13*

Elroi – the God who sees. The God who watches over you.

Hagar was a woman who was thrust into a life of captivity as a young Egyptian slave girl to Sarah, wife of Abraham. Abraham and Sarah had been promised by God that they would have a child; but in the course of time, Sarah not wanting to wait any longer on the fulfillment of God's promise to her, took matters into her own hands. As was the acceptable custom of that day, Sarah gave Hagar to her husband Abraham, to produce a child through the young fertile slave, and the plan was that the child would then be reared as Sarah's thus producing the heir and fulfilling her desire to be a mother.

Of course, as is always the way when we take God's matters into our own hands, it didn't work out as Sarah had planned. Once Hagar became pregnant, Hagar became prideful and didn't want to be the submissive slave girl any longer or to give up her son to the other woman. Thinking more highly of herself with the leverage position that she thought this child brought her in Abraham's household, she began to boldly try to take a place of prominence. Jealously between the two women became unbearable. Hagar began to hate her Mistress Sarah and would taunt her with the fact that she was the one who bore Abraham a child and that Sarah was barren which in that day was a shame for a woman, as if she were cursed. Through their pride came envy, strife, and greed to have more of what they each felt they deserved. A battle of jealousy ensued between the two women and Hagar runs away into the desert the first time and is cast away into it the second, where she finds herself both times in a place of hopeless death even worse than the place she was running from. But in that barren dry parched place, Elroi, the God who sees, is there for her. He knew it all before it happened and he had prepared the way for her and for her child. Elroi is here for you too, waiting, watching, seeing all and ready for you to call out to Him in your humbled state of brokenness.

"Pride comes before the fall" - every single time. However, a humble heart will find favor with God. Pride turned outward is called ego. It's saying you think you are the best, the smartest, above others. You don't see the need for a Savior other than yourself. However there is another form of pride that is just as seriously destructive – some call it low self-esteem or insecurity but it's still pride because it is still all about you; the focus is still you. Whether you think you are the best of the best or the worst of the worst, you are still at the forefront of your mind and you are still the center of your universe, your feelings still take center stage.

Self-loathing is sin. Not only are you thinking more about yourself than you ought, either more highly or in this case, more lowly, you are saying to God and others that you don't respect the Image of God that He created in you. You are saying you don't trust God to be able to save you, transform you from your current self to the one He created you to be, and you don't trust Him to use you in the way you were designed to be used. You are saying you don't respect the gifts and equipping He placed in you, not to mention His very breath of life, and you are saying that you selfishly care more about what other people think and feel about you, how you feel about yourself than about how God feels about you.

Under that banner of pride grows other sins that have to be unwrapped and faced as well. When we are dissatisfied with our own lives, we will begin to look out at others around us with envy, believing that they have something bigger, better, more appealing than what we have been given by God and then we greedily want what others have been given rather than appreciating, being thankful for what we have been given. Jealousy, envy and greed will overcome us, bitterness will set in like a poison that infects everything in us and around us, and slowly killing off everything of any true value in our life.

Thank God and appreciate each day in all that it holds.

Write out a gratitude list each day and thank God for each thing no matter how small it may be in the beginning. In doing so, you will suddenly realize you are blessed and highly favored right where you currently are.

<u>Chapter Nine</u>

The slow fade into oblivion was not something I planned. I didn't wake up one morning and say, "Hey, I think I am going to become a full blown drug addict today. In the process, I am going to kill every single relationship I have and hurt everyone who loves me." That is not what happened. In fact, the guilt I felt regarding those relationships every single time I picked up a pipe or a needle kept me going back for more. A crazy, confusing cycle of despair. I jumped on the vicious death spiral completely oblivious to what was to come and I allowed everything negative to rule my thoughts as I sank into despair and further away from reality.

I heard someone say once, "Sin will take you farther than you want to go, keep you longer than you want to stay, and cost you more than you want to pay." That doesn't just include drug addiction. Ask people who have been set free through the love of Christ from pornography, sex addiction, depravity, alcoholism, gambling, the list goes on, and they will tell you that this is a true statement. There is one statement that holds more merit than the one above:

John 8:32 – Then you will know the truth, and the truth will set you FREE.

I *thought* I was free. Free to be ME. Free to live as I chose, to do what I wanted, to make my own choices, how I wanted, when I wanted. How DARE you come at me and tell me I was wrong. Therein lays the ultimate lies of all, the truest forms of deception...DENIAL and PRIDE.

We had gotten pregnant again in a drunken attempt to fix our broken relationship. We were desperate to make things right between us and sex just seemed like the normal thing to do to come back together. We immediately went from black and white (no grey area here) and jumped clear from one extreme to another with more questions than answers.

First came the sickness, then the exhaustion, then the little white stick with its double pink lines that mocked me. I had been living with a so-called "friend", a dope buddy on her best days, and decided to move back into the home I once shared with this man. The horror of September 11, 2001 soon filled up the TV screen as the phone rang incessantly off the hook. Within a matter of hours, I stood alone. I was now a wayward girlfriend of a deployed airman and no one (not even family) knew of our impending baby-to-be.

Oh, how I love excuses. And here was another excuse, another reason to allow paranoia to seep into my vulnerable mind. Drugs were traded for countless, sleepless nights sitting in front of video poker machines in obnoxious casinos. I ostracized every person who tried to befriend me. I allowed the darkness to consume me, and I sank deeper and deeper into a depression that was becoming very hard to mask. I tried desperately to remind myself of who I said I was supposed to be and what I was supposed to act like. Forget what God said. I had lost Him on the trip years before.

I attempted on my good days to model myself after other strong, courageous officer's wives in a vain, narcissistic pursuit to change on the outside what was happening to me on the inside. All that did was add even more shame and guilt to an already heavy weight and it pushed me into the dark hole of lies and further from the Truth.

LIE #9 – **You better get your act together. You aren't fooling anyone. This has now become the most dangerous game you will ever play and you suck at it. Keep playing, though, or everyone will know your secrets and you will be left alone. Your baby inside you doesn't even deserve you. You will never be a woman of character. No one will ever love you.**

TRUTH #9 - IT IS WRITTEN: *"Shout for joy, O daughter of Zion! Shout in triumph, O Israel! Rejoice and exult with all your heart, O daughter of Jerusalem! The Lord has taken away His judgments against you, He has cleared away your enemies. The King of Israel, the Lord, is in your midst; You will fear disaster no more. In that day it will be said to Jerusalem: Do not be afraid, O Zion; Do not let your hands fall limp. The Lord your God is in your midst, a victorious warrior. He will exult over you with joy, He will be quiet in His love, He will rejoice over you with shouts of joy. I will gather those who grieve about the appointed feasts – they came from you, O Zion; the reproach of exile is a burden on them. Behold, I am going to deal at that time with all your*

oppressors, I will save the lame and gather the outcast, and I will turn their shame into praise and renown in all the earth. At that time I will bring you in, even at the time when I gather you together; Indeed, I will give you renown and praise among all the people of the earth, when I restore your fortunes before your eyes, says the Lord" Zephaniah 1:14; 3:14-20

Romans 5:1-9 - Therefore, having been justified by faith, we have peace with God through our Lord Jesus Christ, through whom also we have obtained our introduction by faith into this grace in which we stand; and we exult in hope of the glory of God. And not only this, but we also exult in our tribulations, knowing that tribulation brings about perseverance; and perseverance, proven character; and proven character, hope; and hope does not disappoint, because the love of God has been poured out within our hearts through the Holy Spirit Who was given to us. For while we were still helpless, at the right time Christ died for the ungodly. For one will hardly die for a righteous man; though perhaps for the good man someone would dare even to die. <u>But God demonstrates His own love toward us, in that while we were yet sinners, Christ died for us. Much more then, having now been justified by His blood, we shall be saved from the wrath of God through Him.</u>"

Secrets are the enemy's way of keeping you bound and under his control. He does not want you to know that God loves you or that other people love you. He wants you to believe you are the most unlovable person and that if they see you for who you really are, they will cast you out so you begin to avoid people, isolate, not have others as the voice of reason but hear his accusations which become your truth. Secrets require that lies be told to cover them. Secrets give power to fear. Secrets divide us from other people so we can never fully engage in relationships because we are always afraid they will find out the things we have tried to hide from them.

Trying to keep your sin a secret is maddening. It paves the way to more sin, more hiding, more fear. Under the cover of darkness, the enemy will destroy your life.

As one Woman of God I know so often says, we only have two choices when it comes to our sin, "you either come clean or you stay away nasty". Come to Jesus and be cleansed.

> *Nahum 3:10-12, 19 - Yet she became an exile, she went into captivity; also her small children were dashed to pieces at the head of every street; they cast lots for her honorable men, and all her great men from the enemy. All your fortifications are fig trees with ripe fruit – when shaken, they fall into the eater's mouth. There is no relief for your breakdown, your wound is incurable. All who hear about you will clap their hands over you, for on whom has not your evil passed continually?*

Exposure to The Light of God's Word of Truth is the only way to stop the madness that this secret keeping brings on. The Bible tells us in 2 Corinthians 12:10 that in admitting our weakness, Christ is made strong. So when we admit we are powerless over a problem and that God is all powerful over that problem, we actually are released from the burden and find strength and peace. Rather than hide your weaknesses, your sins, your pain, take it to the Lord in prayer and trust Him with the outcome. He is faithful.

Julie's Own Words of TRUTH:

Revelation 3:8 - I know your deeds. See, I have placed before you an open door that no one can shut. I know that you have little strength, yet you have kept my word and have not denied my name.

This past year has truly been a test, a laboratory of sorts. One thing after another has come against me, yet I still walk toward my purpose even when I am weak. So many days I have longed to stay in bed and sleep until the cows come home. So many days I have refused to put pen to paper, yet I did it anyway. So many times I have wanted to give up, throw my hands in the air and hide in a corner, but I didn't.

My assumption is that I can go anywhere and do anything with my unseen Creator as my guide. People of science and atheism who say there is no proof of God have their own hypothesis. Well, I also have mine. A hypothesis is a tentative assumption made in order to draw out and test its logical consequences, an interpretation of a practical situation or condition taken as the ground for action. I have always had a scientific mind, one that requires proof. So where is that proof? In the Word of course.

God isn't some big man in the sky checking off a naughty or nice list. He is so close, and of course He knows my every move. If He knows my every move, then He also knows the struggles I face, the thoughts that race, what happens before, during, and after I awake. He knows the fear, the triumphs, the mountains, and the valleys. He knows the exhaustion, the love, the discord, and the doubt. HE KNOWS ME. God created me before time and knew my purpose.

Psalm 139:1-24 - You have searched me, Lord, and you know me. You know when I sit and when I rise; you perceive my thoughts from afar. You discern my going out and my lying down; You are familiar with all my ways. Before a word is on my tongue You, Lord, know it completely. You hem me in behind and before, and You lay Your hand upon me. Such knowledge is too wonderful for me, too lofty for me to attain. Where can I go from Your Spirit? Where can I flee from Your presence? If I go up to the heavens, You are there; if I make my bed in the depths, You are there. If I rise on the wings of the dawn, if I settle on the far side of the sea, even there Your hand will guide me, Your right hand will hold me fast. If I say, "Surely the darkness will hide me and the light become night around me," even the darkness will not be dark to You; the night will shine like the day, for darkness is as light to You. For You created my inmost being; You knit me together in my mother's womb. I praise You because I am fearfully and wonderfully made; Your works are wonderful, I know that full well. My frame was not hidden from You when I was made in the secret place, when I was woven together in the depths of the earth. Your eyes saw my unformed body; all the days ordained for me were written in Your book before one of them came to be. How precious to me are Your thoughts, God! How vast is the sum of them! Were I to count them, they would outnumber the grains of sand — when I awake, I am still with You. If only you, God, would slay the wicked! Away from me, you who are bloodthirsty! They speak of You with evil intent; Your adversaries misuse Your name. Do I not hate those who hate You, Lord, and abhor those who are in rebellion against You? I have nothing but hatred for them; I count them my enemies. Search me, God, and know my heart;

test me and know my anxious thoughts. See if there is any offensive way in me, and lead me in the way everlasting.

What am I to do with this proof that comes from the Word of God, this assumption that I can make which has been tested for generations? It is grounds for action. What actions are required for me to walk through the open door? What is on the other side? Does it really matter as long as it is in His will? All I have to do, even in my weakness, is WALK, because He sees, and He knows. As Pastor Charlie Haynes always says, "The end of something is always the beginning of something else."

Revelation 21:6 - He said to me: "It is done. I am the Alpha and the Omega, the Beginning and the End. To the thirsty I will give water without cost from the spring of the water of life.

Chapter Ten

The battle ensued as days forgotten turned into weeks lost to depravity. Weeks spent crying out from a body that had long ago given over control to the darkness, screams being emitted from a soul gone astray, but never permeating the ears of anyone who would listen. Weeks turned into months, months into years; and by now, two young boys were growing up in complete dysfunction.

Gone were the days of youth. I couldn't even look at my worn out self when passing by mirrors and even if I stole a glance, I saw distortion as if I were looking at myself through a funhouse mirror.

James 1:23-24 - Anyone who listens to the word but does not do what it says is like someone who looks at his face in a mirror and, after looking at himself, goes away and immediately forgets what he looks like.

We moved away after a too close call with the authorities (which would prove not to be my last), an empty bank account, and we flew on the wings of doubt to a new and improved location. It was another geographical cure at best, one that worked for a little while until those nasty demons started knocking at my front door. I willingly let them in and then blamed everyone but the President it seems for my new lot in life that was familiar but much more dangerous and much more destructive.

I found myself hooked on dope again and wandering the streets searching for chaos in one of the most dangerous cities on the planet, Washington D.C.

What I saw, the things I subjected myself to, the fear in the faces of lost people wandering around this God-forsaken planet with no purpose and no desire to see the light of day; souls confused and uncaring, hiding from the light, moving in dark shadows through the night. God was not there…but was He?

Matthew 25:30 - And throw that worthless servant outside, into the darkness, where there will be weeping and gnashing of teeth.'

Many, many mistakes led to many, many near fatal consequences. I found myself frequenting dark and dingy anonymous rooms where people are enticed to know of a higher power that long ago had been forgotten to be Jesus Christ Himself through years upon years of traditions and laws that promised "freedom" without a Savior. His name was hidden behind self-liberty. I was then enslaved to 12 steps and self-help. I uttered loud boasts from pulpits designed to keep me in bondage so I still became entangled in my flesh when I would look upon the wondering and curious faces of innocent children who loved me unconditionally. Guilt would then rob me of my peace and I would pick back up where I left off and my condition would be worse than before.

I couldn't escape "jails, institutions, and death…oh, my". My higher power, which was the anonymous room itself, couldn't save me. I lost everything I held dear. To look upon my face would break anyone's heart, if they had a heart to understand my pain. My eyes were lonely, empty, and dark; and the soul inside the frame of the horrible human shell had all but given up. Jails, institutions, and death…oh, my.

The sound of bars clanging, the hard, cold concrete beneath my feet, the cries of the lost and hopeless, the desire to see the Light, the desperation in the sound of my own voice as I clamored for a ray of hope still try to haunt me today.

Then, I begged for God to kill me. I no longer wanted to live inside the barriers of my mind. The walls of my heart began to cave in, inside or outside the boundaries of whatever "institution" I had found myself in. Several moves, three suicide attempts, and a loss that wracked my being to its core was more than I take. I was a dead woman walking.

LIE #10 – You are not worthy to even live on this planet. You have lost everything and your soul is wasting away. Just die already. This is the end for you. You did this to yourself and now there is no one who can save you.

TRUTH #10 - IT IS WRITTEN: *"Bless the Lord, O my soul, and all that is within me, bless His holy name. Bless the Lord, O my soul, and forget none of His benefits; Who pardons all your iniquities, Who heals all your diseases; Who redeems your life from the pit, Who crowns you with lovingkindness and compassion; Who satisfies your years with good things, so that your youth is renewed like the eagle. The Lord performs righteous deeds and judgments for all who are oppressed. He made known His ways to Moses,*

———

His acts to the sons of Israel. The Lord is compassionate and gracious, slow to anger and abounding in lovingkindness. He will not always strive with us, Nor will He keep His anger forever. He has not dealt with us according to our sins, nor rewarded us according to our iniquities. For as high as the heavens are above the earth, So great is His lovingkindness toward those who fear Him. As far as the east is from the west, so far has He removed our transgressions from us. Just as a father has compassion on his children, so the Lord has compassion on those who fear Him. For He Himself knows our frame; He is mindful that we are but dust. As for man, his days are like grass; As a flower of the field, so he flourishes. When the wind has passed over it, it is no more, and its place acknowledges it no longer. But the lovingkindness of the Lord is from everlasting to everlasting on those who fear Him, and His righteousness to children's children, to those who keep His covenant and remember His precepts to do them." Psalms 103:1-18

Psalm 103 shows us God's lovingkindness over every area of our life. There is nothing about us that He does not intimately care about. The original Hebrew word in place of the word "soul" in Psalms 103 is *"hephesh"*, defined as our entire being. What the Psalmist is saying is that we have rest physically, spiritually and emotionally when we commit our life to the Lord. The word "fear" he uses here is an awe of God, a reverent respect.

Psalm 103 ends with Verse 22 telling us "Bless the Lord, all you works of His, In all places of His dominion; bless the Lord, O my soul!" Our soul can be blessed no matter what we have done, no matter how empty we feel now. He says - all you works of His – that is you and me; in all places of His dominion – that is if we surrender our heart and life to God.

What areas of your heart and life are you still trying to hold on to your own dominion over rather than acknowledging God's dominion over them? There cannot be two Kings on the throne of your heart just as a house divided will fall. God will bless your soul, your *hephesh*, your entire life if you surrender control of yourself to Him.

Nahum 1:9-15 - Whatever you devise against the Lord, He will make a complete end of it. Distress will not rise up twice. Like tangled thorns, and like those who are drunken with their drink, they are consumed as stubble completely withered. From you has gone forth one who plotted evil against the Lord, a wicked counselor. Thus says the lord, though they are at full strength and likewise many, even so, they will be cut off and pass away. Though I have afflicted you, I will afflict you no longer. So now, I will break his yoke bar from upon you, and I will tear off your shackles. The Lord has issued a command concerning you: Your name will no longer be perpetuated. I will cut off idol and image from the house of your gods. I will prepare your grave for you are contemptible. Behold, on the mountains the feet of him who brings good news, Who announces peace! Celebrate your feasts, O Judah; Pay your vows. For never again will the wicked one pass through you; He is cut off completely.

JESUS overthrew satan's plot to bind us from our destiny when He went to the cross for us! Hallelujah!!! We just have to believe it and walk in that promise and power, taking back our God-given authority. When the stone was rolled away, Jesus was gone; He had risen. Jesus was victorious in taking back the keys to hell, death and the grave so therefore those of us in Christ, with His all-powerful Spirit in us, we are victorious to overcome all things the enemy attacks us with here on earth while we are here serving our destiny purpose and enjoying the fruits of this life.

This is where your response is critical though. You must recognize your enemy and stand firm in the Truth of God's Word, speaking it out loud in Praise of God and His precious promises to you, His child. Speak out because not only are you hearing and encouraging yourself, but because the devil can't read your thoughts, he has to hear your words that you are claiming the blood of victory over your life under the banner of Your Lord, Jesus Christ.

Hopelessness and depression...those are oppressive attempts by the demonic spirit of suicide to not only bind you from fulfilling your destiny purpose in glorifying God, but a calculated plan of death meant to utterly destroy you.

I want to address a lie that many people believe, that death by suicide *automatically* sends a person to hell. THAT IS ABSOLUTELY NOT BIBLICAL. And while I'm at it I also want to dispel the lie that dying of a drug overdose *automatically* sends a person to hell. THAT IS ABSOLUTELY NOT BIBLICAL.

Apart from Grace there is no way that any human could ever die in a sin free state to allow them access to Heaven. Anything other than grace and we would have to die mid-sentence of saying we are sorry and asking forgiveness. I don't care who you are, how saintly you have behaved all your life or what you have never done – yet. Apart from the Grace of God through the blood covering of Jesus that you have personally yourself at some point entered into covenant relationship with by confessing Him and accepting Him as your Savior, salvation would not happen for anyone. So Sister Sue on the Church Pew can be just as lost as a goose, and Brother Beau the Hobo may actually be saved.

Sin is sin. It is all disobedience to God and yes, God hates sin, some He even names as abominations because of their destructive power over His beloved creations, but He loves the person and it is His will that all come to repentance and be reconciled to Him. We humans do not know the hearts of other humans. Only God knows the heart. Only God knows if a person has ever truly made that blood covenant with Jesus; so only God knows if that person is saved or not when they die. We don't know the full circumstance of anyone's heart or life and we cannot judge others by the sin they commit or the mistakes they make.

The Bible, God's infallible Word tells us that there is only one unpardonable sin. All others can be covered under the blood of Jesus no matter how bad you, I, or anyone else thinks they are. Jesus paid the price for all sin that we ever commit, past, present, and future. We humans can fall out of fellowship with Him, getting off focus, allowing the things of the world to creep back in, monopolizing our time and clouding our decisions, taking us off in the opposite direction sometimes, places we never intended to go, just as we do in our human relationships, but the fact that we are His and He is ours, our blood covenant, is still intact, it does not change IF we were truly in a covenant relationship with Him in the first place. IF you were truly saved, you know it in your heart and nothing changes that inner core love bond with Him.

The Bible makes it very clear that there is only one sin in which we cannot find forgiveness and that is to blaspheme the Holy Spirit of God. Blasphemy is a sin of hate from deep within the heart. The Holy Spirit is the One who draws us to Christ for forgiveness of our sin and to enter a love relationship with Him. If we hate the Holy Spirit, denying His power, and turn our back on Him, never listening to Him or following Him as He beckons us to Jesus for salvation, as He convicts us of our Sin to bring us to salvation repentance, as He leads us to Christ to enter covenant. That blasphemous hate in our heart for Holy Spirit, refusing to ever acknowledge or act upon His calling us to Christ, that is the unpardonable sin taking us to the place of the damnation of our soul with an eternity spent in a real lake of fire, burning in hell, where there is weeping and gnashing of teeth from the souls crying out in agony apart from God.

Over the course of serving in grief ministry, I have talked with several people who have agonized and could not find peace in the death of a loved one because no matter what relationship the deceased had ever once had with the Lord, they believed the lie that their loved ones suicide or drug overdose were unpardonable sins. This is just another trick of the enemy to destroy not only the

---

person, but everyone connected to them. God is not the author of confusion. Go to God's Word for Truth. Don't believe something just because a human Preacher said it from a pulpit. Go to the WORD!

The demonic spirit of suicide very often moves from one generation to the next systematically devising a plan to destroy. Just like in Julie's case with mental anguish over the death, the circumstances surrounding the death, the what-ifs, and the lies; look at the lingering effect it had on her. The tormentor has not stopped trying to destroy her as well as her own children by using her resulting self-destructive behaviors and beyond. Rather than carry the glory of God from parent to child, through one family member to the next, the pain, shame, and guilt of her father's demise rendered his daughter ineffective at best in fulfilling her destiny purpose for many years of her life.

Believing the lies that came from the oppressive spirit, Julie, like so many children caught in the aftermath of a parent's death, had feelings of loneliness and emptiness, rejection, abandonment, fear, shame, and even self-loathing, causing her to isolate from others, those who loved her most, because she felt so unlovable and unworthy. In the isolation is where the enemy could heap on more destruction and death by keeping her blinded from a loving relationship with God. In doing so, he also kept her from a loving Christ-centered relationship with her spouse and her children, preventing her from rearing her children, that next generation, in the ways of the Lord. The enemy very nearly succeeded in destroying Julie's life, BUT GOD!

Psalm 105:8 - He has remembered His covenant forever, The word which He commanded to a thousand generations.

Psalm 105:14-15 - He permitted no man to oppress the, and He reproved kings for their sakes; Do not touch My anointed ones, and do My prophets no harm.

You can pull down the strongholds on your life by accepting Jesus Christ as your personal Savior, your means of salvation, making Him the Lord of your life, continually seeking to grow in your faith walk with him, learn about , believe and walk in His promises for you personally and your future generations, praying – talking, listening, spending time daily in an intimate relationship with God, applying God's Word to your everyday life and being thankful in all things with a heart and mouth of praise. With the power of the Holy Spirit of God within you, knowing Who that power really is, and operating in His wisdom, power, & discernment, you can break generational curses, you can renounce and banish the spirit of heaviness, hopelessness, depression, and suicide forever. You can go from victim to victorious!

Bear fruit of the Holy Spirit in you. Whatever you yield your members to, that's what you become a servant of. Pray your weaknesses to the Lord so He can build you up. Use the authority you have as a child of God to put chaos and affliction under your feet in order for you to have shalom – His perfect peace which surpasses all understanding.

Chapter Eleven

` Loneliness, Despair, Unworthiness, LOST...words to describe the condition of my heart when I would wake up in the cold, sterile, washed out environments of hospitals still breathing the breath of life, tubes still down my throat. WHY was I still alive?? A favorite pastor of mine once said, "The end of something is really the beginning of something else". I just wanted it to be the end.

The most painful grief I have ever felt is the heart wrenching pain of a knife cutting so deep through flesh that would soon turn hard from the desire to make the pain go away. This is pain of losing my children and knowing full well that I was to blame. Divorce finally put an end to my marriage due to my negligence and I was quickly ripped of the title "parent" as well. As of this writing, it has been nearly 5 years since I have looked upon their beautiful faces that look like my very own reflection and eyes that share the same hue. I have yet to hear their voices as they quickly become young teenage men and take the slow turn into adulthood.

Every single day I wake up from nights of endless dreams of the two children I brought into the chaos of this world and my heart. I dream of holding them in my arms and singing a new song to their downcast and confused spirits. I spend days pushing back the guilt, only for it to come back up like waves of nausea at the back of my throat. I imagine the gulf of space and time that stands between us and wonder if they will ever desire to know me.

I will never forget the moments surrounding their births, their first cries as I held them in my arms and looked into their perfect faces while their dad witnessed another miracle taking place, the beginning of a new life. I remember seeing God all over that room as I pondered the names I would give them that would reflect us as a family. I knew they were destined for greatness, that they would be smart as whips, charismatic, and full of personality. My sons whom I love with everything I have inside me, who I long for daily, who take up my every waking thought.

My choices led me to this place of emptiness inside, a hole in my heart that can never be filled by another soul. Here is the awful truth – the one thing I desire the most in life is the very same thing that brings forth so much guilt that I want nothing more than to numb myself from the pain. If that isn't lunacy, I don't know what is. Insanity is doing the same thing over and over expecting a different result. Lunacy is doing the same thing over and over again knowing the end result.

The song my mom passed down to me, the one I remember her singing so softly as she put us to bed each night as a child, is the same song that I used to sing to my boys as they fell asleep, trusting me that all would be well. The lyrics may be familiar to you:

"You are my sunshine, my only sunshine.
You make me happy, when skies are grey.
You'll never know, dear,
how much I love you.
Please don't take
my sunshine away.

The other night, dear, as I lay sleeping,
>I dreamed I held you in my arms.
>>When I awoke dear, I was mistaken,
>>>And I hung my head and cried.

You are my sunshine, my only sunshine.
>You make me happy, when skies are grey.
>>You'll never know dear,
>>>how much I love you.
>>>>Please don't take
>>>>>my sunshine away."

I remember rocking them to sleep and singing that song. I sang them the same lyrics the very night I walked out and did not return.

LIE #11 – See, I told you so. You are not fit to parent anyone. You won't even want to be around children at all out of complete and total fear of hurting them also with your lack of concern for their well-being. You will die alone, no one will want you after this, so don't even try. You should have succeeded in killing yourself. Everyone would have been better off without you and would have forgotten you, no problem.

TRUTH #11 - IT IS WRITTEN: *"But now, this is what the Lord says – He who created you, Jacob, He who formed you, Israel: Do not fear, for I have redeemed you; I have summoned you by name; you are Mine. When you pass through the waters, I will be with you; and when you pass through the* *rivers, they will not sweep over you. When you walk through the fire, you will not be burned; the flames will not set you ablaze. For I am the Lord your God, the Holy One of Israel, your Savior; I give Egypt for your ransom, Cush and Seba in your stead. Since you are precious and honored in my sight, and because I love you, I will give people in exchange for you, nations in exchange for your life. Do not be afraid, for I am with you; I will bring your children from the east and gather you from the west. I will say to the north, Give them up! And to the south, Do not hold them back. Bring my sons from afar and my daughters from the ends of the earth – everyone who is called by my name, whom I created for my glory, whom I formed and made." Isaiah 43:1-7*

Jehovah Nissi – The Lord my Banner.

When God is for us, who can stand against us!

Over and over in the Bible we see God's children in battles for their lives, their land, their families, just as we are today. Like them, sometimes we are the ones causing the problems, sometimes others. Our battles may look somewhat different on the outside, but they are assuredly the same war on the inside.

Romans 7:14-25 - For we know that the Law is spiritual, but I am of flesh, sold into bondage to sin. For what I am doing, I do not understand; for I am not practicing what I would like to do, but I am doing the very thing I hate. But if I do the very thing I do not want to do, I agree with the Law, confessing that the Law is good. So now, no longer am I the one doing it, but sin which dwells in me. For I know that nothing good dwells in me, that is, in my flesh; for the willing is present in me, but the doing of the good is not. For the good that I want, I do not do, but I practice the very evil that I do not want. But if I am doing the very thing I do not want, I am no longer the one doing it, but sin which dwells in me. I find then the principle that evil is present in me, the one who wants to do good. For I joyfully concur with the law of God in the inner man, but I see a different law in the members of my body, waging war against the law of my mind and making me a prisoner of the law of sin which is in my members. Wretched man that I am! Who will set me free from the body of this death? Thanks be to God through Jesus Christ our Lord! So then, on the one hand I myself with my mind am serving the law of God, but on the other, with my flesh the law of sin."

Even though the Israelites saw the miracles and knew what God had done for them, just like us, they would - over and over - turn their backs on Him and go their own way, living in the ways of the world around them, seeking comfort in other gods, living in disobedience, creating yokes of bondage for themselves, and opening themselves up to the armies of the enemy. Remember, they were God's people, like many of us today who have covenant with Him, but we do things our way instead of His way. But unlike us humans, God is faithful with an everlasting love. Yes He allows afflictions and heartache to come to us in order to discipline us and strengthen our character and faith but when we cry out to Him, He will once again come to our rescue and open the door for our relationship with Him to be repaired and deepened.

So often, as God is trying to lead us to our promised land in life, we get in the way of the victory due to our unbelief, our giving up, our lack of understanding in how to fight the battles with Him, rather than our unwittingly joining enemy forces fighting against Him.

Romans 7:6 - But now we have been released from the law, having died to that by which we were bound, so that we serve in newness of the Spirit and not in oldness of the letter.

Galatians 5: 16-17 - but I say, walk by the Spirit, and you will not carry out the desire of the flesh. For the flesh sets its desire against the Spirit, and the Spirit against the flesh; for these are in opposition to one another, so that you may not do the things that you please.

Self-control seems to be a fruit that so many people either want themselves or they sure wish others had it. Self-control is much more than will power. Will power is operating out of our self-will, our limited, flawed human ability. But self-control is operating out of God power, a Spiritual fruit directly related to our relationship with God.

In order to get self-control and operate out of God's power verses will–power, we have to look at the Fruit of the Spirit here in the fifth chapter of Galatians as IT IS WRITTEN.

Galatians 5:22-25 - But the fruit of the Spirit is love, joy, peace, patience, kindness, goodness, faithfulness, gentleness, self-control; against such things there is no law. Now those who belong to Christ Jesus have crucified the flesh with its passions and desires. If we live by the Spirit, let us also walk by the Spirit.

When I learned this my life changed. The word fruit in Galatians is not plural. Each one of the individual fruit work together as one cohesive unit of our heart's condition. Fruit grows and matures in relation to the nutrients they are receiving daily from the vine as do these fruit in us. The first fruit listed is LOVE and the last is self-control. If you want more self-control, you must begin with love and concentrate on learning to Love more. Out of that love will grow each of the other successive fruit until your heart reaches a state of self-control.

God says that the greatest commands He gave us are to Love Him and Love others. He says all of the other commands come out of those two. Truly if you love God the way you should and you love man the way you should, then you will rarely find yourself hurting Him, others, or yourself by sin or poor choices. The more time you spend with God, the more godly wisdom and discernment you will gain also.

If you want more self-control, you must begin with love and concentrate on learning to Love more. Out of that love will grow each of the other successive fruit until your heart reaches a state of self-control.

Chapter Twelve

Sabotage – Deliberately destroy, damage, or obstruct something.

I am my own worst enemy. I make conscious decisions to sabotage the good right before my very eyes. I did not calculate that my own crazy thinking would have me lying down in front of my very own bus. When I allow stressful situations to get to me, my old friends come for an unwelcome visit. Paranoia is the first to arrive, wreaking havoc on my psyche. Then comes in anxiety, confusion, jealousy, anger, fear, pride, and last but not least, doubt.

I made the jump. Finally. I was running an obstacle race and every so often I would come across a hurdle, precisely placed in my path by the enemy, measured carefully in heights and distance. Just like in an actual race, failure to jump over the hurdle by knocking it down intentionally (self-sabotage), going under it (taking the easy way out), or just running around it (unwillingness to change) is cause for disqualification. Sometimes the hurdles are knocked down accidentally and I find myself flat on my face on the all-weather synthetic track trying desperately to figure out how I got there. Did you get that? I said "all-weather" track. I am NOT at a disadvantage just because the tempests of life come through. The track is meant to support me as I run this race called life, regardless of the storms in the fall and winter of my existence. As I ran upon each one I would be able to clearly make out the names painted on the fence section: addiction, unemployment, financial insecurity, doubt, and fear, death of a loved one, illness, relationships, and most recently – co-dependency.

Where did the teammate go? What happened to allow them to make the jump over the hurdle only to turn their head as the race continues to see me just standing at the hurdle? A choice then has to be made, a choice that is never easy. As I stood there; looking at the hurdle, contemplating the hurdle, cussing out the hurdle, kicking the hurdle, pushing the hurdle, getting frustrated with the hurdle, talking to the hurdle, discussing with others about the hurdle; a choice had to be made. They could have stopped their own race and returned me on the other side of the hurdle and found themselves stuck behind the same hurdle they just jumped. They could have begged, pleaded, encouraged, but they could not CHOOSE for me how I run my own race. They could show me how to jump, but they couldn't force me to make the decision to jump. And that is why I, too, was left standing alone. People could not save me.

It took me a long time to realize that drugs and alcohol were not my problem; I had a relationship problem, with everyone. I was deep in "approval addiction" and didn't even recognize it. I did whatever I needed to do to get on everyone's nice list (whether it be the junkie on the street, the drug dealer, friends on the outside, or friends on the inside) and all it got me was a ton of grief. I ended up pushing everyone away, even after the drugs were no longer a problem. I was desperate for love, the kind of love that couldn't come from any human being, yet I was seeking worldly love anyway. I just wanted friendship. I wanted to be friends with the people that were talking about me behind my back right in front of my face. I wanted to befriend those whose hearts were set on their own agendas. I wanted to be friends with those who would gladly stab me in the back, throw me under the bus, and then speak kindness to my face. I was desperate!! Many a tear were cried and for what?!?! So that I could be distracted by the lies of the enemy and not focus on the truth. I was drowning in my self-pity and clawing for some sort of surface where I felt I could stand up again and reclaim my "friends" and in all reality reaching for people that I had no right to reach out to. If I get the idea in my head that everything concerning me and my circumstances and relationships should always be perfect, I am setting myself up for a fall.

Enter in the geographical cures. I was a nomad, moving from place to place, always looking for a way out of my mess. It comes natural to me. We moved a LOT when I was a kid. I think I moved at least 20 times by the time I graduated college, and all in the same town. It was after I graduated college that I realized moving away meant running away. That was when I started with the "Geographical Cure". After mom's accident, running away seemed like the logical choice. So I did. The military was responsible for some moves, but I always left destruction in my wake. After my divorce, moving was the only option, then after my suicide attempts, another move to another state. Always moving, always seeking something, always looking for peace; a place where people didn't know me, a place where I could at least try, a new beginning, and always a new failure.

IT DOESN'T WORK. Why? Because I always took myself with me. My free will and choices put me in bad places. God didn't put me there. Other gods...drugs, alcohol, people, money, work, things, situations; each one representing a different aspect of life...I worshiped them and concentrated on them for personal identity. And I always ended up back in my Egypt, my land of slavery. I got stuck chasing a nightmare because I didn't obey this very simple command to live in the dream.

This is a most painful grief. To see others walk away from me, their backs turned as they leave me behind to fend for myself and knowing that I was the only one to blame.

LIE #12 – Again, you will always be alone, no one to care for you, no one to love you the way you want to be loved. You keep sabotaging every good thing that comes your way and you will never learn. Solitude, Approval, Rejection, and Abandonment will forever haunt you.

TRUTH #12 - IT IS WRITTEN: *"Therefore, since we are surrounded by such a great cloud of witnesses, let us throw off everything that hinders and the sin that so easily entangles. And let us run with perseverance the race marked out for us fixing our eyes on Jesus, the pioneer and perfecter of faith. For the joy set before Him He endured the cross, scorning its shame, and sat down at the right hand of the throne of God. Consider Him who endured such opposition from sinners, so that you will not grow weary and lose heart." Hebrews 12:1-3*

Something powerful God showed me is that the Hebrew word *"Yasta"* is used in several old testament passages where God is directing His people to "go"; to take their promised land. *"Yasta"* means <u>to go forth as to war</u>. We have to fight for the things God has promised us. The enemy in this world doesn't want us to have them.

The Hebrew word *"balak"* is used for "walk" such as where the Bible tells us that certain people, Enoch for example in Genesis 5:24, "walked" with God. *"Balak"* means <u>to go forth</u> and also <u>to go through</u>, to walk <u>as a way of life or conduct</u>. Many times as we walk forward in life even walking with God, we will go through some things.

The Christian's life is warfare. It is our way of life to battle the enemy and take hold of our promised territory, and then to defend that territory so that no ground is ever lost. <u>There is no armor for our back.</u> We cannot live life in retreat position if we ever want the promises of God. We must move forward into the battle, prepared, armed and with purpose in order to take our God promised abundant life. We must walk this life out with God, always going forth as into battle to claim our Victory!

Ephesians 6:10-20 - Finally, be strong in the Lord and in the strength of His might. Put on the full armor of God, so that you will be able to stand firm against the schemes of the devil. For our struggle is not against flesh and blood, but against the rulers, against the powers, against the world forces of this darkness, against the spiritual forces of wickedness in the heavenly places. Therefore, take up the full armor of God, so that you will be able to resist in the evil day, and having done everything, to stand firm. Stand firm therefore, having girded your loins with Truth, and having put on the breastplate of righteousness and having shod your feet with the preparation of the Gospel of peace; in addition to all, taking up the shield of faith with which you will be able to extinguish all the flaming arrows of the evil one. And take the Helmet of salvation, and the sword of the Spirit, which is the word of God. With all prayer and petition, pray at all times in the Spirit, and with this in view, be on alert with all perseverance and petition for all the saints. And pray on my behalf, that utterance may be given to me in the opening of my mouth, to make known with boldness the mystery of the gospel, for which I am an ambassador in chains; that in proclaiming it I may speak boldly, as I ought to speak."

1 Peter 4:1-2 - Therefore, since Christ has suffered in the flesh, arm yourselves also with the same purpose, because he who has suffered in the flesh as ceased from sin, so as to live the rest of the time in the flesh no longer for the lusts of men, but for the will of God.

Julie's Own Words of TRUTH:

I cut myself off from the one thing that could actually save me. I sat in isolation with my little gods and wondered why in the world I couldn't get it right. I had forgotten that logic never undresses in front of pain. Sometimes God digs ditches in our valleys, so bad has got to get worse because bad was just not deep enough and it was not anything you did wrong. Sometimes things need to look utterly impossible so that God can say, 'I couldn't do it until I knew that you saw no way on earth it could be done.' I trust the promise but I have to survive the process. My process is not the same as Suzie Q or Janey L. I am Julie and God is in CONTROL of MY PAIN and MY

PROCESS just like He is in control of THEIR PAIN and THEIR PROCESS.

You know, I have heard so many times these words, "Give it time" in regards to relationships. What does that mean exactly? Time for what? Time for forgiveness which should be immediate? Time for healing? Time for God to move when He is already speaking? Did we so easily forget that we are only here for such a brief moment in time compared to eternity and we are never guaranteed tomorrow? What time? When I hear those words, it makes me cringe. It means to me that person no longer wants to be in my life and they are, in fact, leaves falling off a branch. And I REFUSE to beg one more person to stay in my life.

You know, the hardest thing I have ever had to learn is that when people walk away, let them leave. Sometimes people only come into our lives for a brief season, they are meant to only serve a purpose that sometimes we can't see or understand. It's not for us to understand. Leaves change with the seasons and fall away before a new leaf is formed. Branches look strong but can only support so much weight before they bend and break in the winds of change, and roots are there for a lifetime, helping to sustain, uphold, and strengthen the tree. The problem we face is when we put lifetime expectations on seasonal people and we try to make leaves into roots. We want desperately for people we care about, trust, and love to stay in our lives forever, but it isn't always so.

Proverbs 13:20 - Whoever walks with the wise becomes wise, but the companion of fools will suffer harm.

Proverbs 22:24-25 - Make no friendship with a man given to anger, nor go with a wrathful man, lest you learn his ways and entangle yourself in a snare.

Ephesians 4:29-32 - Let no corrupting talk come out of your mouths, but only such as is good for building up, as fits the occasion, that it may give grace to those who hear. And do not grieve the Holy Spirit of God, by whom you were sealed for the day of redemption. Let all bitterness and wrath and anger and clamor and slander be put away from you, along with all malice. Be kind to one another, tenderhearted, forgiving one another, as God in Christ forgave you.

Isaiah 59:1-2 – Surely the arm of the Lord is not too short to save, nor his ear too dull to hear. But your iniquities have separated you from God; your sins have hidden his face from you, so that he will not hear.

Romans 5: 1-5 - Therefore, since we have been justified through faith, we have peace with God through our Lord Jesus Christ, through whom we have gained access by faith into this grace in which we now stand. And we boast in the hope of the glory of God. Not only so, but we also glory in our sufferings, because we know that suffering produces perseverance; perseverance, character; and character, hope. And hope does not put us to shame, because God's love has been poured out into our hearts through the Holy Spirit, who has been given to us.

Romans 15:1 - We who are strong ought to bear with the failings of the weak and not to please ourselves.

My relationship with God must go beyond EVERYTHING else I could ever want for myself. It needs to affect my relationships with other people, my time, and my resources...all of it!!

My study Bible says there are 3 steps to a right relationship with God *(NIV Life Application Study Bible Copyright by Zodervan)*:

1. Drop all excuses and self-defense
2. Stop trying to hide from God
3. Become convinced that God's way is better than my way.

Psalm 146:1-5 - Praise the Lord.
Praise the Lord, my soul.
I will praise the Lord all my life;
I will sing praise to my God as long as I live.
Do not put your trust in princes,
in human beings, who cannot save.
When their spirit departs, they return to the ground;
on that very day their plans come to nothing.
Blessed are those whose help is the God of Jacob,
whose hope is in the Lord their God.

Praise the LORD...not humans. I know who my roots are and where they are planted, but CHRIST is the ONLY ONE who truly sustains me. He is my water, my breath, my life. Trust not in humans who fail, who choose to separate the social and spiritual needs of people. God is the hope for eternity!

Hebrews 12:1-3 - Therefore, since we are surrounded by such a great cloud of witnesses, let us throw off everything that hinders and the sin that so easily entangles. And let us run with perseverance the race marked out for us fixing our eyes on Jesus, the pioneer and perfecter of faith. For the joy set before Him He endured the cross, scorning its shame, and sat down at the right hand of the throne of God. Consider Him who endured such opposition from sinners, so that you will not grow weary and lose heart.

<u>*Lisa's Epilogue*</u>

As you can see from Julie's testimony here, we are all on a continual journey in life, ever-changing; a journey where heartache and pain, just as joy and peace are all a part of that journey. While God hasn't promised us an easy life, He has promised us that strength, joy, peace and grace, abundant life can all be found and lived out in Christ through all circumstances of that life.

Grief, while a complex and painful process of mourning the disappointments and losses in our life, can also actually shows us how very much alive we are, and that we do have some measure of love and faith in our hearts. The fact that we grieve shows us we do really care, we have been blessed in life to have known love, that we do have hopes, dreams & desires, and that we do have a need for something more, something and someone outside of ourselves. If we didn't, we wouldn't feel anything when they were gone or long for companionship from others. And yes, although our hearts hurt when disappointments come, tragedy strikes or people are no longer with us, God is so faithful to step in, just waiting for us to seek Him for Comfort. He is here watching, waiting to bring us His peace that surpasses all understanding, the Comfort we so desperately need, and also then to begin the process to redirect and restructure our lives toward the next leg of our travel. It's through His comfort that we can begin to open our heart up for other people and other dreams to now become the next part of our journey.

In the testimony of Julie's journey with multiple compilations of loss, pain and suffering, whether brought on by her own actions or at the hands of others, she experienced grief and many years of it without resolution bringing on more grief.

From the shock and denial at stage one, the enemy started firing away with his weapon of choice, the lie. With each successive painful twist as Julie traveled into stage two, pain and guilt, he fired away with the ugly arrows of more lies. Then as she lay there in agony, stage three came and went, over and over she would experience anger and bargaining – blaming God, blaming herself, blaming others, then trying to make sense of it all, trying to make deals with whomever could just make the pain & reality of life go away.

Then drawing back the enemy fired another deadly blow hoping to use stage four, the depression, reflection and loneliness that came to keep her stuck there long enough while his special forces, the suicide spirit could talk her into putting hand to handle and ending it all.

But here comes Christ with His Light of Truth to bring Julie, myself, and countless others out of the darkness and into His marvelous Light. There was a stage five, the upward turn, even as the enemy lies keep coming, firing away, taking Julie deeper and deeper into her self-destruction, the Holy Spirit was at work, drawing her, giving her an awareness that this was not meant to be her end. Holy Spirit was tapping into that measure of faith that God had deposited into her and each of us in our initial creation, drawing her to Christ to save her life, body, mind and spirit.

It was through that relationship found with Christ Jesus that Julie, I, and countless others all have gone from victims to victorious. Upon accepting Jesus as our Savior and actually surrendering our lives to Him as Lord, Master over our lives, we have found the strength to step out in faith in order to make the upward turn. We are continuing this journey called life walking it out with our Lord in reconstruction, working through, acceptance and hope. We have gone from that gut wrenching pain and fear in the darkness to peace and joy in the Light.

The Lies will still come as long as there is the enemy of our souls, but today the lies are recognized through study of God's Word, time spent in relationship building with Him, talking and listening, yielding to His will, and through fellowship with other believers as there are strength in numbers, to encourage one another.

Today the lies are replaced with Truth, with a new understanding that when we draw close to God, He draws close to us. Today my Name is Victory with faith building strength and endurance to go the distance.

God loves you and we love you, Keep walking

<u>*Julie's Epilogue*</u>

God is not on the pages in the book of Esther, nor was He on the pages of my book for a very long time. It doesn't mean He wasn't there, producing and directing a show, setting me in places I never thought I would be.

Esther was the most unlikely candidate for Queen. She was the wrong nationality, and she even had to hide her true identity, but she was called to save a nation from annihilation and she had FAVOR. Esther becoming Queen was nearly impossible, just like my situation looks impossible, but God lavishes in the impossible because He then gets all the glory. He uses me now, not because of me, but in spite of me.

Esther 2:12-14 - Before a young woman's turn came to go in to King Xerxes, she had to complete twelve months of beauty treatments prescribed for the women, six months with oil of myrrh and six with perfumes and cosmetics. And this is how she would go to the king: Anything she wanted was given her to take with her from the harem to the king's palace. In the evening she would go there and in the morning return to another part of the harem to the care of Shaashgaz, the king's eunuch who was in charge of the concubines. She would not return to the king unless he was pleased with her and summoned her by name.

I fell short and was not qualified to go where God is leading me, but I was called anyway. The names of the past that I answered to on a daily basis still ring in my ear; however, today I hear God calling my name and His voice overshadows the rest and resounds in my heart and spirit. He calls me by the name which He announced to the heavenly angelic host the day I was created for His purpose.

Isaiah 43:1-3 - But now, this is what the Lord says — he who created you, Jacob, he who formed you, Israel: "Do not fear, for I have redeemed you; I have summoned you by name; you are mine. When you pass through the waters, I will be with you; and when you pass through the rivers, they will not sweep over you. When you walk through the fire, you will not be burned; the flames will not set you ablaze. For I am the Lord your God, the Holy One of Israel, your Savior; I give Egypt for your ransom, Cush and Seba in your stead.

I am NOT your girl, your trash, or a loser. I am not someone to be stepped on or stepped over. I am not your enemy, or a figment of your imagination. I am NOT a hopeless addict or a helpless drunk, a lost cause, or your pitiful excuse. I am not someone to feel sorry for. I AM a mother, a daughter, a sister, and a friend. I AM an author, a speaker, a leader, and a trusted servant of the Living God. I am a minister. I am a child of the King! I am a disciple, a friend of Jesus, and a warrior ready for battle!

Isaiah 49:1-3 - "Listen to me, you islands; hear this, you distant nations: Before I was born the Lord called me; from my mother's womb he has spoken my name. He made my mouth like a sharpened sword, in the shadow of his hand he hid me; he made me into a polished arrow and concealed me in his quiver. He said to me, "You are my servant, Israel, in whom I will display my splendor."

I heard a voice from heaven as my name was called, "And He who sits on the throne said, 'Behold, I am making all things new'. And He said, 'WRITE, for these words are faithful and true.'" (*Revelation 12:5*)

It's not what I am called, but what I answer to, and MY NAME IS **VICTORY**!

About the Authors

Julie Keene Ballard is the author of Coming Full Circle Blog at **www.comingfullcircleblog.com**. She has Co-Authored a book entitled, "Open the Doors, See All the People, "Just Susan - #BrandNewKindaFree", and has written a 90 day devotional entitled "#JWGIRL4LIFE – Where the Light Meets the Dark" She is a redeemed addict who was saved by Christ from the streets that desperately tried to consume her.

Julie is currently living in the panhandle of Texas, leading Bible studies online and volunteering at the church she attends. She uses her gifts and talents that God has bestowed upon her to help other anointed Pastors fulfill their lifelong dreams and callings and has published countless books for Pastors nationwide through her newest venture, Full Circle Consulting and Publishing of which she is Founder and CEO.

Julie can be reached via email at **info@juliekeene.com**.

Lisa McCaskell Daughdrill is a born-again Christian, wife, mother, daughter, sister, friend and ordained Minister, from Picayune, MS.

Lisa serves alongside her husband, David, as co-Pastors and Founders of Grace House Ministries, Grace House Transitional Home, a second-phase addiction recovery mentoring program, and Good Grief, Christ centered support groups and bible based grief recovery program.

In addition, Lisa is an Evangelist, Writer, & Bible Teacher, who loves sharing God's Amazing Word with others. Also, wherever she can, Lisa serves with her husband in the mission field with disaster relief, Native American, and other mission work as the Lord leads them.

Lisa earned her Bachelor of Science degree in Biblical Studies from Covenant Bible College and Seminary, Tallahassee, FL, and has a Master's Degree in Theology.

Lisa's life mission is to share the gospel of Jesus Christ with a lost and dying world, to teach others there is deep fulfillment to be had in intimate relationship with Jesus, and to spread the truth of God's Word, that there is hope and healing in Christ just as she and countless others have found who previously struggled with grief, addiction, and more. Lisa wants the whole world to know: God loves you and she loves you! Keep Walking!

Lisa Daughdrill welcomes the opportunity to share her Lord. She can be reached via email: **lisa5058@gmail.com**

PRAYER
OF
SALVATION

"Father, I know that I have broken your laws and my sins have separated me from you. I am truly sorry, and now I want to turn away from my past sinful life toward you. Please forgive me, and help me avoid sinning again. I believe that your son, Jesus Christ died for my sins, was resurrected from the dead, is alive, and hears my prayer. I invite Jesus to become the Lord of my life, to rule and reign in my heart from this day forward. Please send your Holy Spirit to help me obey You, and to do Your will for the rest of my life. In Jesus' name I pray, Amen."

Psalm 40:2 - He lifted me out of the slimy pit, out of the mud and mire; he set my feet on a rock and gave me a firm place to stand.

www.ingramcontent.com/pod-product-compliance
Lightning Source LLC
LaVergne TN
LVHW051412080426
835508LV00022B/3042